CAMBRIDGE   MUSIC   HANDBOOKS

Beethoven: *Pastoral Symphony*

CAMBRIDGE MUSIC HANDBOOKS

GENERAL EDITOR Julian Rushton

Cambridge Music Handbooks provide accessible introductions to major musical works, written by the most informed commentators in the field.

With the concert-goer, performer and student in mind, the books present essential information on the historical and musical context, the composition, and the performance and reception history of each work, or group of works, as well as critical discussion of the music.

Other published titles

Bach: The Brandenburg Concertos MALCOLM BOYD
Bach: Mass in B Minor JOHN BUTT
Beethoven: *Missa solemnis* WILLIAM DRABKIN
Beethoven: Symphony No. 9 NICHOLAS COOK
Berg: Violin Concerto ANTHONY POPLE
Berlioz: *Roméo et Juliette* JULIAN RUSHTON
Chopin: The Four Ballades JIM SAMSON
Debussy: *La mer* SIMON TREZISE
Handel: *Messiah* DONALD BURROWS
Haydn: *The Creation* NICHOLAS TEMPERLEY
Haydn: String Quartets, Op. 50 W. DEAN SUTCLIFFE
Janáček: *Glagolitic Mass* PAUL WINGFIELD
Mahler: Symphony No. 3 PETER FRANKLIN
Mendelssohn: *The Hebrides* and other overtures R. LARRY TODD
Mozart: The 'Jupiter' Symphony ELAINE SISMAN
Musorgsky: *Pictures at an Exhibition* MICHAEL RUSS
Schoenberg: *Pierrot lunaire* JONATHAN DUNSBY
Schubert: *Die schöne Müllerin* SUSAN YOUENS
Schumann: Fantasie, Op. 17 NICHOLAS MARSTON
Sibelius: Symphony No. 5 JAMES HEPOKOSKI
Strauss: *Also sprach Zarathustra* JOHN WILLIAMSON
Stravinsky: *Oedipus rex* STEPHEN WALSH

Beethoven: *Pastoral Symphony*

David Wyn Jones
University of Wales, Cardiff

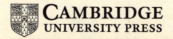

CAMBRIDGE
UNIVERSITY PRESS

Published by the Press Syndicate of the University of Cambridge
The Pitt Building, Trumpington Street, Cambridge CB2 1RP
40 West 20th Street, New York, NY 10011–4211, USA
10 Stamford Road, Oakleigh, Melbourne 3166, Australia

First published 1995

Printed in Great Britain at the University Press, Cambridge

A catalogue record for this book is available from the British Library

Library of Congress cataloguing in publication data
Jones, David Wyn.
Beethoven, Pastoral Symphony / David Wyn Jones
p. cm. – (Cambridge music handbooks)
Includes bibliographical references and index.
ISBN 0 521 45074 8 (hardback). – ISBN 0 521 45684 3 (paperback)
1. Beethoven, Ludwig van, 1770–1827. Symphonies, no. 6, op. 68, F major. I. Series.
ML410.B4W96 1996
784.2'184–dc20 95–9937 CIP MN

ISBN 0 521 45074 8 hardback
ISBN 0 521 45684 3 paperback

AH

For my parents, who first bought me a score of the
Pastoral Symphony

Contents

List of illustrations   *page* viii

Acknowledgements   ix

1 *The concert of 22 December 1808*   1

2 *Background*   4

3 *Genesis and reception*   25

4 *Design and orchestration*   47

5 *Technique and image*   54

6 Mehr Malerei als Empfindung   81
  Some critical views

Notes   89

Select bibliography   96

Index   98

Illustrations

1   Sketch for the beginning of the *Pastoral Symphony*   *page* 26
from the Eroica Sketchbook (1803)

2   A performance of Haydn's *Creation* in March 1808.   31
Miniature by Balthasar Wigand

3   Orchestral part used in the first performance of the   44
Pastoral Symphony (Gesellschaft der Musikfreunde,
Vienna)

Acknowledgements

Many people have given freely of their time and expertise in the preparation of this volume and it is a pleasure to thank them, while at the same time absolving them of any responsibility for the use I have made of their expertise: Otto Biba, David Charlton, Geoffrey Chew, Else Radant Landon, Nicholas Marston, and Meinir Waite. Gill Jones and her colleagues in the Music Library at the University of Wales, Cardiff were eager and efficient in pursuing sometimes quite elusive source material. As General Editor of the series Julian Rushton pointed out many infelicities in the typescript and Malcolm Boyd was an equally punctilious reader of the proofs. Finally, my wife, Ann, and daughter, Yolande, grew used to my exploring the pastoral life alone and at odd times of the day and night; I thank them for their support and encouragement.

A note on editions

It is astonishing to have to report that a good modern edition of the *Pastoral Symphony* is not readily available. The most accessible publications, the miniature scores published by Eulenburg and Universal Edition, contain many errors, including an incorrect title for the first movement and faulty tempo headings for the slow movement and the trio. These scores are derived in the main from the old *Beethoven-Gesamtausgabe* (Serie 1, Nr. 6; ed. Julius Rietz; 1862), published by Breitkopf and Härtel, and most modern performances use orchestral parts taken from this source.

The principal source for the old complete edition was the printed score issued by Breitkopf and Härtel in May 1826; the many interesting readings in the autograph, early manuscript copies of the score, early manuscript performance parts and the orchestral parts printed in May 1809 are undervalued or ignored. Some of these details are incorporated in recorded performances by the London Classical Players (Roger Norrington), Orchestre

Révolutionnaire et Romantique (John Eliot Gardiner) and others. But a fully documented printed score will have to await the publication of the symphony in the new complete edition (*Ludwig van Beethoven: Werke: Neue Ausgabe sämtlicher Werke*, Munich and Duisburg, 1961–).

1

The concert of 22 December 1808

Perhaps the most remarkable concert in Beethoven's career was that given in the Theater an der Wien on 22 December 1808. On a bitterly cold night and with insufficient rehearsal an *ad hoc* ensemble of instrumentalists and vocalists provided a concert of Beethoven's music that lasted from 6.30 to 10.30.[1] Eight works were included in the programme, described on the handbill as follows.[2]

First part

I   Pastoral Symphony, (No. 5) more the expression of feeling than painting.
      First movement. Pleasant feelings which are awakened in mankind on arrival in the country.
      Second movement. Scene by the brook.
      Third movement. Joyful fellowship of country folk; leading into
      Fourth movement. Thunder and Storm; in turn leading into
      Fifth movement. Beneficent feeling after the storm joined with thanks to the deity.
II   Aria, sung by Miss Killitzky.
III Hymn with Latin text, written in the church style, with chorus and solos.
IV Piano Concerto played by himself (Industrie-Comptoir).

Second part

I   Grand Symphony in C minor (No. 6).
II   Holy, with Latin text, written in the church style, with chorus and solos.
III Fantasy on the piano alone.
IV Fantasy on the piano, which gradually includes the orchestra, and ultimately ends with the entry of the chorus as a finale.

Erste Abteilung

I   Pastoral-Symphonie, (No. 5) mehr Ausdruck der Empfindung als Malerei.
      1stes Stück. Angenehme Empfindungen, welche bei der Ankunft auf dem Lande im Menschen erwachen.
      2tes Stück. Scene am Bach.

1

3tes Stück. Lustiges Beisammensein der Landleute; fällt ein
4tes Stück. Donner und Sturm; in welches einfällt
5tes Stück. Wohltätige, mit Dank an die Gottheit verbundene Gefühle nach dem Sturm.

II   Arie, gesungen von Dem. Killitzky.
III   Hymne mit latein. Texte, im Kirchenstile geschrieben, mit Chor und Solos.
IV   Klavier-Konzert von ihm selbst gespielt (Industrie-Comptoir).

Zweite Abteilung

I   Grosse Symphonie in C moll (No. 6)
II   Heilig, mit latein. Texte, im Kirchenstile geschrieben, mit Chor und Solos.
III Fantasie auf dem Klavier allein.
IV Fantasie auf dem Klavier, welche sich nach und nach mit Eintreten des Orchesters, und zuletzt mit Einfallen von Chören als Finale endet.

Each part opened with a new symphony, the *Pastoral Symphony* (at this stage called No. 5) and the C minor (labelled No. 6), two lengthy but very different works that would have tested the musicianship and perseverance of even the most devoted of Beethoven's players and listeners. While the presentation of these two symphonies was the principal aim of the concert Beethoven took the opportunity of pressing his credentials as a pianist-composer, now, because of increasing deafness, a secondary aspect of his career in comparison with ten years earlier; the first part ended with a performance of the Fourth Piano Concerto, recently published by the Viennese firm of Bureau des Arts et d'Industrie (hence the reference in the handbill). The penultimate item in the concert – 'Fantasy' – was an improvisation by Beethoven, the content of which can only be guessed at; almost certainly it was more extravagant than the Fantasy in G minor (Op. 77) composed the following year, which has the feeling of a salon piece rather than something designed to capture the imagination of a large audience. Interspersed between these works were three vocal numbers. The second number, the 'aria', was the oldest item in the programme, the concert aria, 'Ah! perfido' (Op. 65) dating from 1796, though it is possible that this was its first performance in Vienna; it had been published in 1805. For more recent vocal music Beethoven had a number of works from which to choose: the oratorio *Christus am Oelberge* (Op. 85), the opera *Leonore* (Op. 72) and the Mass in C (Op. 86). The opera and the oratorio were already known to the Viennese (both had been given their first performance in the city) and the subject matter of the latter was specifically suited to Easter rather than Christmas; the Mass in C, however, had been given its first performance in Eisenstadt (in September 1807) and was unknown in Vienna. Performances of liturgical music in concerts were still very rare in the city and the Imperial and Royal censor was sensitive about advertising performances of such works outside the church. The oblique references on the handbill to a 'hymn' and movements 'written in the church style' were designed to get round this sensitivity; the two movements were the Gloria and Sanctus. The final item, the Choral Fantasia (Op. 80), brought together all the forces used in the concert in a new work composed at the last moment; it concluded with the massed forces – piano, chorus and orchestra – proclaiming the power of music, 'So, lovely spirits, accept the gifts of fair art gladly. When love and strength are wedded, divine grace is man's reward' ('Nehmt denn hin, ihr schönen Seelen, froh die Gaben schöner Kunst. Wenn sich Lieb' und Kraft vermählen, lohnt den Menschen Göttergunst').

The concert was a compelling statement of Beethoven's creative imagination at almost exactly half way through his life: two radical symphonies, a piano concerto that was quite unlike its predecessors, vocal and instrumental music that showed a willingness to respond to extra-musical stimulus and, above all, the steadfast appeal of traditional genres. The two very different symphonies, one abstract and intensely dramatic, the other avowedly programmatic and relaxed, point to some of the characteristics that were to dominate symphonic composition for over a hundred years. But, as often with Beethoven's music, their subsequent history and reputation have to a large extent obscured the impulses that first produced them.

The *Pastoral Symphony* has been part of the standard repertoire from 22 December 1808 to the present day, though admiration for the work is, at least in part, sustained by a general reverence for the composer rather than by the perceived quality of the work itself. Of all Beethoven's symphonies perhaps the *Pastoral* is the one that needs rescuing most from the cultural icon we call 'Beethoven'. What kind of work did the composer imagine the *Pastoral Symphony* to be? What were the various stimuli that influenced its composition? How might the audience have reacted in December 1808? Removing the veneer of time is a familiar metaphor in the period instrument movement; this book hopes to recapture some of the resonances that the period listener might have experienced. Some people will claim that this is unattainable (which, of course, it is), irrelevant to the 1990s and, therefore, misguided. Needless to say the author does not share this reactionary view. At the very least looking at the *Pastoral Symphony* from the late eighteenth century forwards rather than from the twentieth century backwards represents a change of perspective. It might enable us to marvel anew at the work itself.

2

Background

Concert life in Beethoven's Vienna

The concert on 22 December 1808 that included the first public performance of the *Pastoral Symphony* was designed to present to the public the composer's principal output from the previous two or three years. Although public concert life in Vienna at the time was an active one with regular performances of new works, its characteristics made it very difficult for a single composer to be presented to the public on a systematic and regular basis, and the ambitious nature of the concert in the Theater an der Wien in December 1808 is as much a reflection of this background as of Beethoven's lack of practical common sense.

Vienna did not possess a continuing tradition of public subscription concert series such as had long been established in Paris, London, Leipzig and other major European cities, in which a regular body of musicians performed a planned number of concerts every season to a faithful audience. Subscription concerts were certainly known, as Mozart's biography in the 1780s shows, but none became an enduring part of musical life. In the first decade of the nineteenth century Ignaz Schuppanzigh was the main figure who attempted to hold subscription concerts. Following a practice that can be traced back to Mozart's Vienna, his concerts were held in the Augarten in the summer months, from June to September. Beginning, remarkably, at 7.00 in the morning they lasted for about two hours and featured a mixed programme of vocal and instrumental music. Amateurs were encouraged to join in the performances as soloists and orchestral players, and the whole enterprise was rather casual and lacking in ambition; the programmes never included first performances of major works. Of Beethoven's music, his piano concertos, played by Czerny, Ries and Josepha Auernhammer but never by the composer, and the *Prometheus* overture were performed.[1]

More ambitious was the subscription series held in the winter season of

1807–8, a year before the *Pastoral Symphony*. Usually referred to as the Liebhaber Concerte (Amateur Concerts), but also termed the Musikalisches Institut (Musical Institute), Freunde der Tonkunst (Friends of Music) or Gesellschaft von Musikfreunden (Society of Musical Friends), an organization of seventy members presented twenty concerts between November 1807 and March 1808.[2] The statutes of the organization make it clear that the members aimed to offer concerts of high artistic standards, in content and in performance. Amateur players (especially string players) were welcome but only if they were of sufficient ability; the orchestra was to have a regular membership of fifty-five named players; the customary single rehearsal prevalent throughout Europe was to be held no more than two days before the concert, because a longer interval would prove detrimental to the performance; and for particularly difficult pieces two rehearsals were to be held. After the first concert, which was held at the Mehlgrube, the organization moved to a larger venue, the hall of the university. The twenty concerts of the inaugural series were dominated by two composers: Mozart, fourteen of whose works were performed, and Beethoven, with a total of eleven performances, including two of the First Symphony (17 January 1808 and 20 March), two of the Second Symphony (12 November 1807 and 22 February), two of the *Eroica Symphony* (6 December 1807 and 2 February), two of the overture *Coriolan* (13 December 1807 and 2 February) and single performances of the overture *Prometheus* and of the C major piano concerto (31 January 1808). The final concert of the season, on 27 March 1808, was a performance of Haydn's *Creation*, a celebration of the composer's imminent seventy-sixth birthday and a tribute to Vienna's leading musical figure. The success of this particular concert and of the series as a whole could well have led to a second series in the following winter, but the uncertain political and economic situation resulting from the latest developments in the Napoleonic wars conspired to scupper any such plans.

For Beethoven's reputation in Vienna the subscription series of 1807–8 was clearly highly significant. Shortly before the beginning of the series a Viennese correspondent for the Leipzig journal *Allgemeine musikalische Zeitung* had noted that Beethoven's existing symphonies (Nos. 1–4) were still quite unknown in Vienna.[3] The Liebhaber Concerte rectified that situation in a systematic and comprehensive way. Beethoven, more than any other person, must have entertained hopes of a second series, which would have provided a continuing platform for more recent works. In this ideal world the Fifth and Sixth symphonies would have been given their premieres at separate concerts in the 1808–9 season, with perhaps repeat performances too. As it was,

Beethoven was forced to fall back on the well-established practice in Vienna's concert life, organizing a one-off concert.

Single concerts were of two types, charity concerts and concerts for the benefit of the organizing musician. The concerts of the Tonkünstler-Societät were the most venerable. Founded in 1771, the concerts were held at Easter and Christmas to raise money for the widows and orphans of musicians. The principal fare was usually one or more vocal items, though concertos and symphonies by Viennese composers were often played too. Beethoven had made his public debut as a pianist and composer at a Tonkünstler-Societät concert in March 1795, but over the next twelve years Beethoven the pianist never appeared again and Beethoven the composer was represented by two performances only, the variations on 'Là ci darem la mano' for two oboes and cor anglais (WoO 28) and the Quintet (Op. 16).[4] Other charities that raised money through concerts included the St Marx Bürgerspital (a hospital for the poor) and a general charity called the Wohlthätigkeitsanstalten. These were joined by increasingly numerous concerts to raise money for the victims of the Austrian military effort in the Napoleonic wars. In the first few years of the century Beethoven's name is once again conspicuous by its absence; then in the years 1807–10, as if mirroring the success of the Liebhaber Concerte, his symphonies and concertos feature more often in charity concerts.[5]

Like other musicians who wished to make an impact in Vienna, Beethoven was forced to organize his own concerts, arranging the hire of the venue, securing the musicians, printing the tickets and placing the advertisements. At best a time-consuming process, it was usually aggravated by delays, changes of plan and last minute crises. Before the big concert in 1808 Beethoven had arranged two similar presentations of his music: the first had been on 2 April 1800 at the Burgtheater and had contained the first public performances of the Septet (Op. 20) and the First Symphony; the second was at the Theater an der Wien on 5 April 1803 when the oratorio *Christus am Oelberge*, the C minor piano concerto and the Second Symphony were given for the first time.

From this summary of Viennese public concert life in the first years of the nineteenth century it appears that until the Liebhaber Concerte and some contemporary charity concerts Beethoven's symphonies (and, to a lesser extent, his concertos too) were infrequently heard. Given this background, the vast ambition of the concert on 22 December 1808 has almost an air of desperation about it. Beethoven must have felt that another opportunity was not likely to arise for some years.

If public concert life in Vienna in the first decade of the nineteenth century lacked many of the characteristics that made it central to musical life in other

European cities, the vitality of its private concert life was still unmatched. The part played by the socially and economically privileged members of society in Beethoven's career has always been recognized: the unswerving devotion of Emperor Franz's youngest brother, Archduke Rudolph (1788–1831), the patronage of the established aristocracy such as the Lobkowitz and Lichnowsky families and the support of members of the new meritocracy such as the banker Würth. In the middle decades of the eighteenth century many aristocrats had supported full-time orchestras that had nurtured and developed the symphonies of Haydn, Dittersdorf, Pichl, Vanhal and others; by Beethoven's time very few aristocrats maintained orchestras with the simple consequence that far fewer symphonies were composed. Instead, aristocratic patronage was mainly directed to supporting Beethoven as a teacher, pianist and a composer of piano and chamber music. Nevertheless, two patrons played significant roles in Beethoven's career as a symphonist.

In 1804 and 1805 Baron von Würth, a banker, sponsored private orchestral concerts in his house on Sundays featuring the music of Haydn, Cherubini, Peter Winter, Anton Eberl and, most notably, Mozart. During the winter of 1804–5 the first performance of Beethoven's *Eroica Symphony* was given at one of these concerts.[6] Much more dynamic and central to Beethoven's eventual success as a symphonist was Prince Joseph Franz Maximilian Lobkowitz (1772–1816). His importance has always been recognized but the full extent of Lobkowitz's enthusiasm for music and his lavish indulgence of this interest have become evident only in the last few years through the work of scholars working in the vast family archives in Roudnice (Raudnitz) in the Czech Republic.[7] For Lobkowitz indulged his passion for music in a way that recalls Prince Nicolaus Esterházy, Haydn's main patron, but with an additional recklessness that led inexorably to financial ruin in 1814.

Beethoven's first recorded concert appearance was at the Lobkowitz palace in Vienna in 1795, and in the same year the prince's name appears on the subscription list for the publication of the composer's Op. 1, three piano trios. Lobkowitz spoke German, Italian, French, Czech and a little English, had a bass voice good enough to take the part of Raphael in a private performance of Haydn's *Creation*, and played the violin and cello. In 1797 he formed a small retinue of court musicians under the leadership of Anton Wranitzky (1766–1820), comprising eight string players (sometimes fewer) and three singers. To this core, additional players and singers were hired as necessary. Moving on a regular annual pattern from Vienna, to Prague, to Eisenberg and Raudnitz, and then back to Prague and Vienna, the musicians performed at private concerts, birthday and nameday celebrations, and balls. Oratorios and operas too were regularly given, including Haydn's *Creation* and *The Seasons*, and Mozart's *Die Entführung aus dem Serail* and *Così fan tutte*. Voluminous quantities of music in manuscript and printed form were systematically ordered from Vienna. Extravagant though the patronage was, it was not mere vainglory since Lobkowitz's support was often practical and strategic too. Beethoven, Abbé Vogler, Paer and Hänsel were only four of many composers readily rewarded with payments by Lobkowitz; he was an active member of Gottfried van Swieten's Gesellschaft der Associirten that promoted the late oratorios of Haydn and other choral works; he was a member of the consortium that ran the court theatres for a year; and, most well known, he was one of the three leading enthusiasts for Beethoven's music (Prince Kinsky and Archduke Rudolph were the others) who in 1809 guaranteed the composer an annuity of 4000 florins per annum that enabled him to stay in Vienna.

Beethoven's music was systematically acquired by the Lobkowitz court. In December 1804 Prince Lobkowitz sponsored a private run-through of the *Eroica Symphony* and the Triple Concerto which enabled Beethoven to adjust and revise his scores. The following January Lobkowitz underwrote the costs of including the *Eroica Symphony* in Würth's concert. Two years later the prince organized a series of concerts in his Viennese palace devoted to the music of Beethoven, including all four symphonies, arias from *Leonore*, a piano concerto (probably No. 4) and the first performance of the *Coriolan* overture. This Beethoven 'festival' was a notable private forerunner of the Liebhaber Concerte the following winter and it is no surprise that Lobkowitz was one of the four aristocrats active in the founding of that series.

Beethoven had already acknowledged Lobkowitz's patronage through the dedication of the Op. 18 quartets, the *Eroica Symphony* and the Triple Concerto; he was to be further rewarded with the dedication, shared with Count Razumovsky, of the Fifth and Sixth Symphonies. The part that Lobkowitz played in the early history of the *Pastoral Symphony* will be told in Chapter 3.

Beethoven's reputation and the Viennese musical repertoire

The zealous efforts of Würth and, especially, Lobkowitz to promote the composer, and the founding of the Liebhaber Concerte in 1807 only for it to fold after one season, suggest a concert life that thrived in private but lacked distinction in public. This is confirmed by a report in an issue of the *Vaterländische Blätter für den oesterreichischen Kaiserstaat*. Writing in 1808 an anonymous contributor, who could well have been touting for the Liebhaber Concerte, wrote of the city's musical life:

In this capital, few houses will be found in which this or that family does not entertain itself with a quartet or with a piano sonata and, thanks be to Apollo, the once so despotically widespread card playing has fallen out of fashion. . . Yet so much is devoted to so-called chamber music that there is little opportunity for full orchestral works, for symphonies, concertos etc.[8]

Table 1 gives the number of known public performances of symphonies in Vienna between 1800 (the premiere of Beethoven First Symphony) and 1810.[9]

Between 1800 and 1806 no more than two Beethoven symphonies per year were performed, in 1801, 1802 and 1806 none. Then in 1807 and 1808, largely as a result of the Liebhaber Concerte, there is a surge to four performances and then to twelve. In 1809 and 1810, reflecting the general decline in cultural activities due to the threat of invasion and subsequent occupation by the French, the number of symphonies performed falls back to one and two respectively. Clearly the concert in the Theater an der Wien at the end of 1808 marked the end of a period of intense public exposure for Beethoven's symphonies.

Table 1 shows that only two other composers of symphonies featured with any regularity, Haydn and Mozart. Neither was a modern symphony composer, Haydn having written his last symphony in 1795 and Mozart in

Table 1. Symphonies performed in Vienna in 1800-10

	Haydn	Mozart	Beethoven	Others
1800	7 plus	2	1	–
1801	6	–	–	Eybler (1), Gyrowetz (1), Müller (1), Kauer (1)
1802	2	–	–	Martini (1), Seyfried (1)
1803	3	1	2	Kauer (1), Kramer (1)
1804	1	2	1	Eberl (2), Müller (1), Vogler (1)
1805	3	3	1	Eberl (1), Karnavich (1)
1806	2	–	–	Hoffmeister (1), Kanne (2), Rösner (1), Schacht (1), Tomášek (1)
1807	2	1	4	Cherubini (1)
1808	–	–	12	Fränzel (1)
1809	3	–	1	Moscheles (1), Struck (1)
1810	1	–	2	Rössler (1), Mayseder (1)

1788. In these crude statistics there is already a palpable sense of the Viennese Classical School, the great triumvirate of Haydn, Mozart and Beethoven, emerging. Of the twenty-one other composers whose symphonies were played, only one threatened to rival Beethoven. Anton Eberl (1765–1807) was, in many ways, a similar figure to him. Five years older than Beethoven he began to figure in Vienna's musical life towards the end of the 1780s as a pianist and as a composer. A concert tour of Germany in 1795–6 was followed by a two-year period in St Petersburg, where he conducted the first performance in Russia of *The Creation*. He returned to Vienna in 1802 and soon established a formidable reputation as a pianist and composer; his piano compositions included several sonatas and small piano pieces, three concertos and a double concerto. Two symphonies earned him particular regard, one in E♭ (probably dating from 1803) and one in D minor (1804/5). Following a concert in January 1804 devoted almost entirely to Eberl's music a reviewer in the *Allgemeine musikalische Zeitung* singled out the E♭ symphony for special praise.

A big new symphony by Eberl, dedicated to Prince Lobkowitz . . . is extraordinarily successful, full of bold and new ideas . . . After the first, beautifully worked-out but very long Allegro in E flat comes a splendid Andante in C minor in which the wind instruments are beautifully employed . . . The finale in E flat shows genuine originality and artistic merit. May this symphony soon be made generally available through publication and may Herr Eberl further employ his talents in this genre.

A couple of years later another report in the *Allgemeine musikalische Zeitung* held Eberl's two symphonies to be more satisfactory than Beethoven's *Eroica*. Eberl's position as a continuing rival to Beethoven in the symphony and concerto was not to be maintained however; he died in 1807 at the age of forty-one after contracting scarlet fever.[10]

As well as being the most frequently played of symphony composers in the first years of the new century, Haydn was also the composer of two single works that were unrivalled in their popularity, *The Creation* and *The Seasons*. *The Creation* had received its first semi-private performances under the aegis of Swieten's Gesellschaft der Associirten in April 1798, but its first public performance a year later marked the beginning of what can only be described as a phenomenon in Vienna's musical life. Thirty-one further performances of the work took place in the city up to 1808, usually to raise money for charity and, up to 1802, normally directed by the composer.[11] The number of performances far exceeds that of any symphony and, indeed, most operatic works of the time. Musical life was dominated by the work and its success prompted the composition of a sequel, *The Seasons*, first performed in April 1801. Although this oratorio never achieved the frequency of performance of *The Creation* and Haydn himself thought it an inferior work, it notched up ten further public performances between 1801 and the end of 1808.[12] Like every other musician in Vienna Beethoven could not ignore the popularity of these two oratorios. He once remarked of the Septet, probably his most popular composition, "That is my *Creation*". A more positive response was the decision to compose his own oratorio, *Christus am Oelberge*, first performed at Beethoven's concert on 5 April 1803. It is a much shorter work than either *The Creation* or *The Seasons*, lasting some thirty-five minutes only, and its subject matter, a meditation on Calvary, recalls another oratorio by Haydn, his own adaptation of *The Seven Last Words*, also frequently performed at the time. Beethoven composed the work very quickly and though it received a respectable number of performances in the following years he came to regard it as a weak work, an assessment that posterity has been willing to accept.

The longer term response to the success of *The Creation* and *The Seasons* was more fruitful, for rather than trying to emulate Haydn's success with his own oratorio, Beethoven responded with deepening humility to the subject matter of the works. Both oratorios present a careful mixture of description of natural phenomena with praise and thanks, controlled by the unfolding of the days of the week in *The Creation* and the timeless tread of spring, summer, autumn and winter in *The Seasons*. A list of descriptive passages in the oratorios would run to several dozen items, from the overwhelming portrayal of the first light in *The Creation* to the delightfully trivial chirping of the grasshopper in *The Seasons*. Many pictorial incidents have direct equivalents in the *Pastoral Symphony*. Beethoven's *Scene am Bach* recalls the second part of Raphael's aria in Part I of *The Creation*, 'Leise rauschend gleitet fort im stillen Thal der helle Bach', 'Softly purling through silent vales the limpid brook'. Both have a persistent triplet accompaniment ($\frac{12}{8}$ in Beethoven, $\frac{4}{4}$ in Haydn) representing the chattering flow of the brook, while a slow-moving melody evokes the course of the stream and the overall tranquillity. Beethoven's movement culminates in the celebrated depiction of the nightingale, quail and cuckoo on flute, oboe and clarinet respectively. In the first aria of Part II of *The Creation* Gabriel (soprano) describes in succession the flight of an eagle and the song of the lark, dove and nightingale, all reflected in the orchestral accompaniment and the coloratura vocal line (Haydn and Beethoven, however, have a different perception of the nightingale). The quail makes an appearance at sunset in *Summer* from *The Seasons*, with the same dotted rhythm and instrument (oboe) as in the Beethoven, but not the same pitch ('D' in Beethoven, 'G' in Haydn). Beethoven's third movement, *Lustiges Zusammensein der Landleute*, most recalls the boisterous wine chorus in *Autumn*, 'Juhe, juhe, der Wein ist da' ('Bravo, bravo, the wine is here'); both movements incorporate dances and become increasingly unruly. A brief storm, with specific depictions of wind, lightning and rain, occurs in Part I of *The Creation* in an accompanied recitative, but a more powerful precursor of Beethoven's storm in the *Pastoral Symphony* is the chorus in *Summer*, 'Ach! das Ungewitter nah't' ('Hark! the storm approaches'), which has the same power and might of Beethoven's storm as well as the details of lightning, wind and thunder. Haydn's storm is in C minor, Beethoven's in F minor, and both portray the reluctant subsiding of the storm, turning eventually to the major key. Indeed the initial layout of Beethoven's movement strongly suggests a chorus, the 'voices' entering in b. 21 and 'singing' the material given thereafter to the wind instruments. Beethoven's storm moves directly into the last movement, *Hirtengesang: Frohe und dankbare Gefühle nach dem Sturm*. This has a direct counterpart at the beginning of *Summer*, 'Der muntre Hirt versammelt nun die frohen Herden' ('The cheerful shepherd gathers now his joyful flock'). Heard side by side the similarities are striking: F major, $\frac{6}{8}$, solo horn, a melody in arpeggio pattern, pedal points with consequent superimposition of tonic and dominant chords, and a sense of an introduction that leads to a song, sung by Simon in *The Seasons*, first violins in the *Pastoral Symphony* (Ex. 1a and b).

As well as these programmatic elements – tranquil, comic and dramatic – Beethoven's symphony shares with Haydn's two later oratorios the same overwhelming sense of awe and inner contentment promoted by the unforced majesty of nature, whether it is Raphael's aria towards the end of Part II of *The Creation* that surveys the universe at the conclusion of the fifth day ('Nun scheint in vollem Glanze der Himmel', 'Now heaven in fullest glory shone'), the first chorus of peasants in *The Seasons* ('Komm, holdner Lenz des Himmels Gabe, komm', 'Come, gentle Spring, O gift of Heaven, come'), or the first movement of the *Pastoral Symphony* (*Erwachen heiterer Empfindungen bei der Ankunft auf dem Lande*, *Awakening of happy feelings on arrival in the country*). In Haydn's oratorios this skilful blend of description and contemplation leads inevitably to climactic choruses of praise; in *The Creation* most occur at the end of the day, a pattern also discernible in *The Seasons*. Beethoven's symphony has the same ineluctable sense of moving towards affirmation, the *Hirtengesang*. Although Beethoven makes no mention of the time of day in his symphony there is the implication that the *Ankunft* (from

Example 1a

Example 1b

the city), the brook, the revelry, the storm and the song of the shepherds are all within one day, from morning through mid-afternoon to late evening. In that sense the symphony is as fundamentally satisfying as any of the explicit days in *The Creation* and *The Seasons*.

There is nothing in Beethoven's correspondence, in the voluminous sketches for the work and in the anecdotal heritage that directly links the composition of the *Pastoral Symphony* with the Haydn's oratorios, yet the richest testimony of all, the music itself, strongly suggests that the symphony was Beethoven's long term response to the popularity of the works in Vienna and beyond. A third oratorio on a pastoral subject would have risked limiting Beethoven's responses and would inevitably have promoted comparison with Haydn; a symphony was a more strikingly individual tribute, both to the subject matter and to the composer who had dictated the course of symphonic development in the second half of the eighteenth century.

One consequence of writing a symphony rather than an oratorio was that the pictorial element had to be kept in control. One wonders whether Beethoven contemplated and subsequently rejected certain images for his symphony such as an autumn or winter landscape, a hunt (plenty of symphonic precedents there), sunrise or sunset. Certainly, like Haydn, Beethoven would have been aware of the long tradition of the pastoral in music.

The pastoral tradition

Although the immediate stimulus of Haydn's late oratorios was the determining one, Beethoven joined Haydn in evoking pastoral images in ways that can be traced back to the Renaissance; they were only the latest composers to explore a deep rooted part of human psychology using musical techniques that were honoured by time. Few commentators on the *Pastoral Symphony* avoid mentioning its place in the broad history of the pastoral in music, drawing attention to the stylistic features that constitute the *lingua franca* of such music: pedal points (or in a mannered context, drone basses), compound time, piping melodies, repetition and measured delivery of material. For modern listeners works such as Corelli's *Christmas Concerto*, Vivaldi's four concertos *The Seasons*, Handel's *Messiah* and Bach's *Christmas Oratorio* are easily associated with Beethoven's symphony. But these works represent only the best-known of an extensive repertoire of music of all kinds that constitutes the pastoral tradition.

In 1923 Adolf Sandberger published a valuable article on the long historical background to Beethoven's symphony.[13] Listing dozens of composers and works, this article remains an impressive catalogue of the pastoral tradition, beginning with the chanson and frottola of the medieval period, noting its importance in the Renaissance madrigal, and documenting the extraordinary burgeoning of the tradition in the Baroque period in opera, oratorio, mass, cantata and all kinds of instrumental music. As a metaphor for idealized emotions the pastoral extended from the robustly rustic, even vulgar, to the elevatingly Christian. As well as the generalized musical fingerprints noted above, the pastoral often included more specific pictorial images too: birds of all kinds, but especially the cuckoo, hen, nightingale and turtledove; storms on land and on sea, often with the ensuing calm; and waterscapes of all kinds (seas, rivers and brooks). Sandberger prefaces his article with a quotation from Goethe's *Propyläen*: 'If one wants to speak of a splendid work of art, it is necessary to discuss the entire art, for the work encompasses it all.' Given that the pastoral tradition is nowhere near as pervasive in nineteenth- and twentieth-century music, Beethoven's symphony is indeed a cumulating point to over three hundred years of tradition.

As to the mundane question of how much of this legacy Beethoven was directly familiar with, the realistic answer would be very little indeed. In later life the composer became interested in older music, from Palestrina to Bach and Handel, but at the time of the composition of the *Pastoral Symphony* his likely knowledge of composers from previous epochs extended only to keyboard music by Bach and some oratorios by Handel. But there is no need to couple pastoral movements in Bach and Handel with Beethoven's *Pastoral Symphony*, because musical life in German-speaking Europe in the second half of the eighteenth century affords plenty of instances of the continuing tradition of the pastoral in music, instances that conditioned Beethoven's responses in his symphony and help to explain the effect it had on contemporary listeners who could not bring to mind the music of Monteverdi, Vivaldi, Bach and Handel.

Beethoven's players and his immediate public in Vienna would have encountered the pastoral most readily in church music of the time. There was a strong tradition of pastoral masses, works by Brixi (1732–71), Eberlin (1702–62), J. A. Kozeluch (1738–1814), Vanhal (1739–1813) and others that featured the usual clichés of pedal points, compound rhythms, piping melodies and deliberately naive phrase patterns.[14] Typically the masses are in G major, avoiding the sound of trumpets and timpani that characterize the predominant tradition of masses in C major. Often entitled *missa pastorale* (or some variant) the works were usually, but not exclusively, performed during Advent. Today, the most familiar example is Haydn's *Missa Sancti Nicolai*, first performed in December 1772. The large number of sources for this work shows that it was regularly performed throughout Catholic central Europe from that date to at least the early nineteenth century.

A more homely genre, again associated with Christmas services, was the pastorella.[15] Drawing on the same instrumental and vocal resources as other church music of the time it was cultivated in rural Austria, Bavaria and Bohemia, and set a German text (often in dialect) that related the story of the shepherds in the fields, the visit of the heavenly host, the departure for Bethlehem, and the worship at the crib. The repertoire is typically both comic and enchanting, with folk-like melodies (sometimes actual folksongs), and dumbfounded surprise and alarm alternating with the elevated and the elevating. Unlike the more international Italian pastoral tradition this distinctive Austro-German tradition makes frequent use of short-breathed tunes in $\frac{2}{4}$, as found in the first movement of the *Pastoral Symphony*. The genre title pastorella is distinctive too, replacing the 'pastorale' found in Italian pastoral works; often during the composition of his symphony Beethoven was to use this form in his title ('Sinfonia pastorella') and it appears on the parts used in the first performance.[16] Joseph Haydn, Michael Haydn, Dittersdorf, Hofmann and Vanhal all contributed to this engaging repertory; there is even a pastorella attributed to Beethoven.[17] The very urban Mozart is one of very few composers in the second half of the century who did not contribute to the tradition, though, as Geoffrey Chew has shown, his mature operas show that he was acquainted with it.[18]

A third category of pastoral music encountered in Catholic churches was the Pastoral Symphony. Symphonies and other orchestral music were regularly played in church services in Austria, usually single movements interspersed between the sections of the Ordinary. The title *sinfonia pastorella* (and variants) is reasonably common, whether applied by the composer himself or by a local scribe or cataloguer revealing the context, a church service, in which that particular work was played. Among such works are four by Cannabich (1731–98), four by Leopold Hofmann (1738–93), and one each by Ignaz Beecke (1733–1803), Johann Stamitz (1717–57) and Anton Zimmerman (c. 1741–81).[19] However, the Pastoral Symphony repertoire reveals one important difference from Beethoven's masterpiece. It was not the custom for individual movements to carry programmatic titles and, indeed, individual works such as Hofmann's symphony in D major are sometimes devoid of all pastoral imagery.

16

The programme symphony

Important though the tradition of the pastoral in Catholic church music is to Beethoven's work, he was, of course, writing a symphony for a secular concert and not for a church service. With its several passages of explicit description the *Pastoral Symphony* is more obviously placed in the history of the programme symphony in German-speaking Europe. To a far greater extent than their contemporaries in England, France, North Germany and Italy, composers in Austria, Bavaria, Bohemia and Hungary showed a steady interest in symphonies with a programmatic content.[20] Haydn's trilogy of symphonies from 1761, 'Le matin', 'Le midi' and 'Le soir', and the 'Farewell' symphony of 1772 are only the most familiar of programme symphonies from the period. Sometimes specified emotional states are conjured up (that is making explicit what is normally implicit), as in a C major symphony by Vanhal whose three movements are headed *Speranza* (*Hope*), *Sospirare e Languire* (*Sighing and Languishing*) and, as the finale, *La Lamentazione* (*Lamentation*) moving towards *L'Allegrezza* (*Gaiety*).[21] In other cases the programme is more obvious, as in the six symphonies that Mysliveček (1737–81) wrote on the months of the year from January to June. Recurring subjects for complete symphonies or individual movements include battles, national characteristics, journeys, hunts, weddings and descriptions of the weather, and it is not difficult to find symphonies that anticipate the subject-matter of individual movements of Beethoven's *Pastoral Symphony*.

In 1793 the Viennese composer and publisher Franz Anton Hoffmeister (1754–1812) issued a symphony in F major of his own called *La primavera* (*Spring*), a four-movement work but with no further details of a programme; the first movement has a theme typical of the Austrian pastoral tradition, exploiting the same associations as the first movement of the *Pastoral Symphony* (Ex. 2).[22] The third of Dittersdorf's six extant symphonies from the 1780s based on Ovid's *Metamorphoses* is entitled *Acteon's transformation into a stag*; its slow movement is a picture of the goddess Diana bathing in a stream, the texture of the music (long-breathed melody over repetitive figuration) being the same as that used by Beethoven in the *Scene am Bach*.[23] Leopold Mozart's Symphony in D major, *Die Bauernhochzeit* (*The Peasant Wedding*) describes the progress of a wedding celebration, with instructions for optional pistol shots and whistling during the opening march.[24] Finally, storm movements are common: *La tempesta* in a symphony in E♭ major by Vanhal[25] and the finale of Haydn's *Le soir* (No. 8) are only two of many that could be cited.

Example 2

A distinctively Austrian form of the long tradition of representing bird song in music was the custom of including parts for specially constructed instruments, imitating the hen, cuckoo, quail and nightingale. Leopold Mozart's so-called Toy Symphony (which circulated under the names of Joseph and Michael Haydn too) is a well-known example. As well as a cuckoo part, a symphony by Anton Zimmerman entitled *Pastoritia* includes the sound of an alpine horn, produced by an instrument termed a *tuba pastoritia*.[26]

One work from this substantial repertoire of programme symphonies was given pre-eminence in the nineteenth century when it was claimed as the model for Beethoven's *Pastoral Symphony*: Justin Henri Knecht's *Le portrait musical de la nature*, a symphony in G major composed for pairs of flutes, oboes, bassoons, horns, trumpets and timpani, plus strings. The nineteenth-century Belgian music historian François-Joseph Fétis was the first to draw attention to the similarities between Beethoven's *Pastoral Symphony* and this earlier work, in his celebrated dictionary and in an article published in the *Revue et Gazette Musicale de Paris*.[27] The work is in five movements and was published by the firm of Bossler in Speyer in 1784. The previous autumn the same firm had published three juvenile piano sonatas by Beethoven (WoO 47) and it is assumed that Beethoven would have become acquainted with Knecht's symphony through this mutual publisher. In fact, Beethoven could have renewed his acquaintanceship – or, of course, discovered the work for the first time – in Vienna in the 1790s when manuscript parts of the work were advertised by the firm of Johann Traeg.[28] However, Beethoven's library at the time of his death did not include any kind of copy.[29]

If attempts to prove that Beethoven knew the work are inconclusive, a glance at the work itself will show that the composer would have learnt nothing from it. A descriptive programme is given on the title page.[30]

1. A beautiful landscape where the sun shines, the gentle breezes blow, the brooks flow through the valley; the birds warble, a purling stream descends from a height, the shepherd pipes, the lambs frolic and the sweet voice of the shepherdess is heard.

2. The heavens darken and cloud over; every living thing is breathless and

frightened. Black clouds accumulate, winds whistle, the distant thunder rumbles and the storm slowly approaches.

3. With howling winds and driving rain, the storm breaks in full fury, the treetops groan, the foaming waters rush with a dreadful noise.

4. Gradually the storm subsides, the clouds disperse and the sky clears.

5. Nature, transported with joy, lifts its voice to heaven and gives thanks to the Creator in soft and pleasant songs.

The parallels in the subject matter are clear but otherwise this five-movement structure is not a symphony in the sense that Haydn, Mozart and Beethoven used the word. There are no sonata form movements; rather each movement is a short character piece determind by its programmatic content; moreover, Knecht shows no willingness to merge the programmatic with the symphonic as in the programme symphonies of Dittersdorf, Haydn, Vanhal and others. In short, the work does not warrant being elevated to a position of particular influence. In his Sixth Symphony Beethoven was responding to a pastoral tradition that was both wider and more challenging than is represented by this single work.

Beethoven's love of nature

29 June 1801, letter to Wegeler [31]

You will rent a house for me in some beautiful part of the country and then for six months I will lead the life of a peasant.

c. 4 March 1807, letter to Marie Bigot [32]

The weather is so divinely beautiful – and who knows whether it will be like this tomorrow? – so I propose to fetch you about noon today and take you for a drive . . . the morning is now the most lovely part of the day.

26 July 1809, letter to Breitkopf and Härtel [33]

The whole course of events [i.e. the French occupation of Vienna] has in my case affected both body and soul. I cannot yet give myself up to the enjoyment of country life which is so indispensable to me.

Sometime in May 1810, letter to Therese Malfatti [34]

How fortunate you are to be able to go into the country so soon. I cannot enjoy this happiness until the 8th, but I look forward to it with childish excitement. How delighted

I shall be to ramble for a while through bushes, woods, under trees, through grass and around rocks. No one can love the country as much as I do. For surely woods, trees and rocks produce the echo which man desires to hear.

27 May 1813, letter to Archduke Rudolph[35]

I am convinced that the glorious beauties of Nature and the lovely surroundings of Baden will restore my balance and that a twofold calm will take control of me.

24 July 1813, letter to Archduke Rudolph[36]

To stay in town during the summer is torture to me.

Sometime in March 1815, letter to Joseph Xaver Brauchle[37]

. . . at the present moment my spirit can only feel at ease in the presence of the beauties of nature, and so far I have made no arrangements anywhere else to give free play to this irresistible inclination of mine.

As the above extracts from Beethoven's correspondence show there is ample direct evidence of the composer's love of the countryside. In the winter months he usually lived within the city walls but he habitually took an afternoon walk on the Glacis, the broad strip of land outside the walls that separated the city from the suburbs. In the summer months he resided in one of the villages or small towns that surrounded Vienna: Hetzendorf, Heiligenstadt, Nussdorf, Mödling and, most frequent of all, the spa town of Baden. In these places he could indulge his enthusiasm for long country walks, more often than not alone, the solitude and tranquillity greatly aiding his contentment. Although Beethoven sought relaxation in the summer months they were often, too, periods of ample creativity and many of the composer's significant works, such as the Third and Fourth Symphonies, were composed (or substantially so) when living outside the city. As well as thinking through a particularly pressing compositional issue Beethoven pondered new ideas on his walks. In 1818 the artist August von Kloeber (1793–1864) wrote 'I encountered Beethoven several times on my walks in Mödling, and it was most interesting to see him, a sheet of music paper and a stump of pencil in his hand, stop often as though listening, and then write a few notes on the paper.' The artist subsequently painted a full length portrait of Beethoven in the Mödling landscape, now unfortunately lost.[38]

That Beethoven was acquainted with some contemporary literature on natural history is suggested by a letter written in February 1810 to Breitkopf and Härtel; he asks for assistance in buying a copy of Johann Matthaeus Bechstein's *Naturgeschichte Deutschlands* (*The Natural History of Germany*), which he wants as a gift for an unspecified friend. Beethoven's biographer Anton Schindler drew repeated attention to Christoph Christian Sturm's *Betrachtungen über die Werke Gottes in der Natur* (*Reflections on the works of God in Nature*), stating that the composer owned a dog-eared copy of it and entered many passages in a breviary of favourite quotations, alongside Shakespeare, Homer and Goethe.[39] Sturm (1740–86) was a Lutheran cleric who lived in Magdeburg and Hamburg. His book first appeared in 1772 and was published in several later editions; it was also translated into French and English and regularly printed in those languages throughout the early nineteenth century. For each day of the year, from January through to December, there is a short homily on a seasonal subject matter. In a way that might have reminded Beethoven of the texts of *The Creation* and *The Seasons*, these 'thoughts-for-the-day' give equal importance to the ordinary (18 May, 'Reflections on Grass'), the wondrous (14 April, 'Sunrise') and the uplifting (31 October, 'The Heavens declare the glory of God'). Not surprisingly, some of the homilies have equivalent subject matter in the *Pastoral Symphony*: 4 March, 'Winds and Tempests'; 17 April, 'The Use of Rain'; 22 June, 'The Nightingale' and 8 July, 'Thunderstorms'. Many of the essays move with increasing animation to praising the Creator, the same process, but on a smaller and more intimate scale, found in Haydn's oratorios and in the broad sweep of the *Pastoral Symphony*. The content is homely and comforting rather than penetratingly theological and Sturm's outlook is firmly that of the eighteenth century: mankind assumes his place in a universe in which everything, however large or small, has its function within a perfect system of checks and balances. It is more in this general outlook than in any specific allusion that one senses the spirit of the *Pastoral Symphony*. For a mid-summer's day, 6 July, Beethoven could have read an essay of three paragraphs entitled 'The many enjoyments we find in Nature'. It includes the following.[40]

Let us turn our eyes to whatever part of the creation we please, we everywhere find something that interests either our senses, our imagination, or our reason.

All nature is so formed, as to afford us numberless pleasing objects, and to supply us with a variety of enjoyments, which continually succeed each other. Our constant taste for variety is always gratified. Each part of the day brings new pleasures, either to our senses or to our imaginations. While the sun illuminates the horizon, the plants and animals, with a thousand agreeable objects, strike our eyes; and even in the night we are charmed and transported with the majesty of the sky. Nature seems to labour on every side, to surprise us with new pleasures. We must be blind and senseless indeed, if we are not struck with this infinite variety, and if we do not acknowledge the wisdom and goodness of the Creator. The same spring that waters the valley, quenches our thirst, pleases our ear, and invites us to sleep. The shady forest, which defends us from the heat of the sun, where we hear the melody of various birds, feeds at the same time a multitude of animals, which are themselves food for us. The same trees whose blossoms, a few months ago, delighted our eyes, will soon produce delicious fruits to please our taste; and the fields, now covered with waving corn, will soon supply us with plentiful crops . . .

O let us, who are the happy witnesses of the wonders of the Lord, let us, in the presence of all his creatures, pay constant grateful adoration. All things remind us of his goodness, and shew our obligations to praise him. May our souls be filled with grateful joy.

During the winter months Beethoven would have drawn sustenance from the essay on music, designed to be read on 22 December, which by unnerving coincidence was the date of the concert in the Theater an der Wien in 1808.[41]

From music we derive the purest pleasure we enjoy. It charms the ear, soothes the passions, touches the heart, and influences the temper and disposition; its harmonious accents calm our griefs to silence, revive our spirits, and ennoble the sentiments. Such a pleasing and useful science is worthy of our attention, and should prove another motive to glorify our Creator . . . Let us then bless that God who has enabled us to receive the various impressions which are imparted by sound, and to associate certain ideas with bodily sensations. What various sources of delight he is continually bestowing. Oh! let us express our thanks by glorifying his name, and employ the melodious strains of music to elevate our exulting hearts with gratitude to our great Benefactor.

The pastoral in Beethoven's music

The uniting of the pastoral heritage with Beethoven's love of nature found its greatest single expression in the *Pastoral Symphony* but, after this single all-embracing display, he did not return to the subject matter again. Nevertheless, throughout the composer's life there are a number of movements (or parts of movements) that invoke the topos of the pastoral, often in a sublimated manner: the slow movement of the Septet, the first movement of the late A major piano sonata (Op. 101), the F major bagatelle from the Op. 33 set and the 'Dona nobis pacem' of the *Missa Solemnis*. But only one other movement carries the label pastoral. The tenth movement of the ballet *Die Geschöpfe des Prometheus* (1800–1), first performed seven years before the *Pastoral Symphony*, is headed 'Pastorale'; it is an allegro movement in C major consisting of 101 bars in $\frac{6}{8}$ time with drone accompaniments (octaves at first, later fifths), a tonal design that barely leaves the tonic, and a harmonic language that is overwhelmingly tonic and dominant. Only the broad outline of the plot of the ballet is known and the dramatic reason for the pastoral movement is a matter of conjecture; it must have been the pastoral dance that is mentioned in the broad outline. The immediate context of the movement foreshadows the *Pastoral Symphony*; it is preceded by an agitated movement in C minor that eventually subsides into a *pianissimo* C major, a progression that exactly mirrors that of the storm going into the *Hirtengesang*. However, the C minor movement is unlikely to have been an actual storm because the action of the ballet had opened with *La tempesta*, another C minor movement. The *sforzando* accents, the timpani rolls, the string *tremolo* moving through arpeggio figuration and the lightning figure ♫ ♪ were all to feature in the *Pastoral Symphony*; this movement too subsides into *pianissimo*.

The piano sonata in D major (Op. 28) dates from the same year as the premiere of the ballet and is often called the 'Pastoral' sonata, prompted by the extended tonic pedal that characterizes the opening theme and the $\frac{6}{8}$ finale. But it was not Beethoven's title; it seems to have occured first in the unsanctioned English edition of the work issued by Broderip and Wilkinson c. 1805. Even more removed from an authenticated pastoral content is another contemporary work, the so-called 'Spring' sonata for piano and violin (Op. 24, 1801); the nickname arose after Beethoven's death.

The most notable anticipations of the subject matter of the *Pastoral Symphony* are to be found in a forgotten corner of Beethoven's output, song. Up to the time of the symphony Beethoven had written over forty songs. He was particularly occupied with the medium in the early 1800s, composing new songs or gathering existing ones together for publication, a marked change of emphasis from the solo piano music that had dominated his output up to that time. The eight songs of Op. 52, published in 1805, contain some works that date back to the early 1790s; the three verses of 'Maigesang' (Op. 52, No. 4) unite in pleasant tunefulness the contemplation of nature (the sun, the blossom and the dawn chorus) with young love. The single song 'Der Wachtelschlag' (WoO 129), published in 1804, sees in the insistent call of the quail an invitation to praise and thank a beneficent God. Set in F major, with the same dotted figure as Haydn had recently used in *The Seasons* and Beethoven was to use in the slow movement of the *Pastoral Symphony* (not to mention countless quail passages in Toy symphonies), the song associates the distinctive rhythm of the bird with the text 'Fürchte Gott' ('Fear ye God'), 'Liebe Gott' ('Love ye God'), 'Lobe Gott ('Praise ye God'), 'Danke Gott' ('Thank ye God') and 'Bitte Gott' ('Pray to God'); the second section changes from a $\frac{2}{4}$ larghetto to a $\frac{6}{8}$ allegretto, the birdsong now rendered in lilting rhythms to the words 'Traue Gott' ('Trust in God'). In image, sentiment and musical technique the song is especially close to the *Pastoral Symphony*.[42] The linking of nature and religion, rather than nature with romance, occurs again in a cycle of six songs (Op. 48) on texts by Christian Fürchtegott Gellert (1715–69), published in 1803, though specific musical anticipations of the *Pastoral Symphony* are not found. The fourth and fifth of Beethoven's settings, 'Die Ehre Gottes aus der Natur' and 'Gottes Macht und Vorsehung', are proclamations of God's presence in nature, the nearest Beethoven came to setting one of Christian Sturm's homilies. Predominantly chordal and syllabic, they draw on the same powerful C major tradition that informs 'Die Himmel erzählen' ('The heavens declare') in *The Creation*.

The aesthetic and musical background to the *Pastoral Symphony* is one of the most wide-ranging, diverse and complex of any of Beethoven's major compositions. Apparently more ambitious works, such as the *Eroica* and the Fifth Symphony, draw on a narrower, more focused range of stimulus. The *Pastoral Symphony* explores a series of overlapping resonances: the age-old imagery of the pastoral, but without ever sounding archaic or conventional; the programmatic, without yielding to the narrative or to the trite; and the religious, but without the church and the liturgy. All are contained within the self-sufficient world of the symphony. It was an achievement that drew readily on tradition, even though there was no single precedent for the work; and through this tradition it aimed to engage contemporary listeners rather than to challenge them.

3

Genesis and reception

First thoughts

Many accounts of the genesis of the *Pastoral Symphony* begin in 1803, noting that a sketchbook devoted mainly to the *Eroica Symphony* contains the following sketch (Ex. 3).

Example 3

Gustav Nottebohm was the first to draw attention to this sketch[1] and it was given wider currency though its appearance in the preface that Wilhelm Altmann wrote in 1942 for the Eulenburg minature score (No. 407). The tempo marking, the reference to the brook, the implied incessant triplet motion and the charming throwaway comment 'the deeper the brook, the lower the note' constitute a clear anticipation of the *Pastoral Symphony* completed five years later. It is, in fact, one of several individual references – or concept sketches as Beethoven scholarship has termed such annotations – to the symphony in the volume.

Between the summer of 1803 and the spring of 1804 Beethoven used a sketchbook of about 182 pages mainly for intensive work on all four movements of the *Eroica Symphony*, but also for some work on the 'Waldstein' sonata (Op. 53) and numbers from the opera *Leonore*. A detailed stave-by-stave inventory of the sketchbook by Rachel W. Wade[2] has revealed that over forty works, or potential works, are alluded to in the volume including the Triple Concerto (Op. 56), the Fifth Symphony, *Christus am Oelberge*, many small piano pieces, the aborted opera *Vestas Feuer* and several songs. Some concept sketches were to remain dormant for several years, others were to

Plate 1.   Sketch for the beginning of the *Pastoral Symphony* from the
Eroica Sketchbook (1803)

remain unrealized (including two bars headed 'Symphony in D minor' and
the beginning of a Kyrie movement in A major), while a few cannot be related
to any known or projected work. Obviously those for the *Pastoral Symphony*
belong to the first category. The sketch for the slow movement is found on
p. 96, following over ninety pages devoted almost exclusively to the *Eroica
Symphony*; Wade suggests that it was written before November 1803. Were
it not for the specific verbal references to the brook there would be nothing
to associate it with the slow movement of the *Pastoral Symphony*: it is in the
wrong key (C major, then in an implied F major); it is in alla breve rather than
$\frac{12}{8}$; and the thematic profile (though not the implied harmony) is a long way
from the final product. It would be unwise to dismiss an association with the
symphony, if only because there are other more explicit musical references
to the work elsewhere in the sketchbook, but to regard this single annotation
as the catalyst for the entire work is misguided. It should be acknowledged
that there is nothing in the concept sketch that Beethoven needed to remember
and the extensive sketches for the slow movement that date from 1808 could
have been made without reference to it. Also, the fact that the sketchbook
contains preliminary ideas for three songs of which only the last was ever
completed – 'Zur Erde sank die Ruh' von Himmel nieder', 'Das Rosenband'
(Klopstock) and 'Vom Tode' (Gellert) – suggests that 'Murmeln der Bäche'
might have been an idea for a song rather a symphonic movement.

Three further concept sketches in the volume are more obviously related to the *Pastoral Symphony*. On p. 64 are noted four bars of the melody of the trio section of the third movement (bb. 165–8). But it is written a fifth lower and with a key signature of three flats, which perhaps suggests some unrealized connection with the *Eroica Symphony*. On p. 118 the first seven bars of what was to be the opening of the *Pastoral Symphony* are sketched; there is no tempo indication, it is written in $\frac{4}{4}$ rather than $\frac{2}{4}$ and the instrumentation is given as violas, cellos, horns and bassoons rather than the firsts, seconds, violas and cellos of the final product. The parallel thirds were not part of the final theme, though the sonority is a distinctive one elsewhere in the symphony (Plate 1). On p. 178, on some spare staves in the middle of sketches for the revised version of *Christus am Oelberge*, the crescendo passage into the first tutti and the beginning of the tutti itself are sketched (bb. 34–41); the music is now in $\frac{2}{4}$.

Two further concept sketches in the Eroica Sketchbook could have been associated with the idea of a symphony with a programmatic content. On p. 179 there are seven bars of a $\frac{4}{4}$ melody in F major to which the title *lustige sinfonia* (*merry symphony*) is attached; and on p. 158 two bars of F major music in $\frac{3}{4}$ which is headed *Wald* (*Forest*). In neither case can the melodic content be related to any material in the *Pastoral Symphony*.

The sporadic references to the *Pastoral Symphony* that are contained in this sketchbook reveal more about Beethoven's working practices in general than they do about the real beginning of the work; recognizable snatches of melody and references to 'Murmeln der Bäche' 'lustige sinfonia' and 'Wald' do not constitute a groundplan for a symphony. Nevertheless, the opening melody, that of the trio section and, more tenuously the hints of a symphony with a programme clearly retained their attractiveness over the next few years as the *Pastoral Symphony* began to assume a more definite shape in the composer's mind.

1804–7: establishing the vision

Many of the ideas contained in the Eroica Sketchbook were brought to fruition in works completed in the next few years, including the Triple Concerto, Fifth Symphony, *Leonore* and the 'Waldstein' sonata. Other major works completed between 1803 and 1808 include the Fourth Piano Concerto (Op. 58), the Fourth Symphony (Op. 60), the Mass in C (Op. 86), the Violin Concerto (Op. 61) and the overture *Coriolan* (Op. 62). Except for the mass there are very few extant sketches for these major works and Barry Cooper has suggested that several sketchbooks from this period have not survived.[3] It is possible that these missing sketchbooks devoted to extensive work on any or all of the Fourth Piano Concerto, Fourth Symphony, the Violin Concerto and *Coriolan*, could have contained ideas that later found their way into the *Pastoral Symphony*. Since biographical and other evidence points firmly to 1808 as the time when sustained and committed work was done on the symphony, any ideas in these missing sketchbooks would very likely consist of further concept sketches.

Of the major works completed in the period 1804–7 – an opera, two symphonies, two concertos, a mass and an overture – the temper of two of them, the Fourth Piano Concerto and the Mass in C, comes close to that of the *Pastoral Symphony*. The predominant qualities of the G major concerto, lyricism and restraint, have always been recognized, especially in comparison with the Third and Fifth Piano Concertos. Czerny's account of the work in the chapter 'On the proper Performance of All Beethoven's Works' from *Die Kunst der älteren und neueren Klaviercompositionen* (*The Art of Older and Newer Compositions for the Piano*) characterizes the opening tutti with a string of epithets, including the word pastoral: 'Simple, peaceful, serene, agreeable, almost in the pastoral style'. But, as Czerny's qualification 'almost' indicates, the work is not an exploration of the pastoral and should not be brought into direct relationship with the *Pastoral Symphony*.[4]

A much more promising work in this regard is the Mass in C, composed in the summer of 1807. The work had been commissioned by Prince Nicolaus Esterházy for performance in Eisenstadt to mark the nameday of his wife, Marie Hermenegild. This local tradition was now eleven years old and all but one of Haydn's six late masses had been specially composed for the annual occasion. When in 1802, following the first performance of the 'Harmoniemesse', Haydn retired from the composition of major works, the duty was take over by Hummel and Fuchs, who probably performed masses by other composers as well as their own. Beethoven's Mass in C was not well received at its first performance in September 1807, a reception aggravated, as often in the composer's career, by his paranoia about the commitment of the musicians.

Today, the work suffers in two different comparative assessments that are virtually unavoidable. First, its indebtedness to Haydn's late masses is clear and there is a palpable feeling of a composer writing within himself; it is one of the least ambitious works of the decade. Second, and more damaging, it also suffers in any comparison with the *Missa Solemnis* (Op. 123), even when such striking anticipations of the later work as the forthright beginning of the Gloria and the unorthodox repetition of the text of the Agnus Dei during the 'Dona nobis pacem' are noted. Beethoven himself, however, held the work in great affection: 'it is especially close to my heart' he wrote to Breitkopf and Härtel in the summer of 1808.[5]

Perhaps one reason for this undoubted affection was that the commission, which was unsolicited, encouraged the composer to consider certain expressive and structural concerns that were entirely new, concerns that were to be reflected in the *Pastoral Symphony*. The opening of the mass – a relaxed simple melody in thirds in an unhurried tempo and over a pedal C – is a clear elicitation of the pastoral. This is not a consistent topos in the mass and certainly the work does not warrant the title Missa Pastorella, but the mood returns in the concluding seventeen bars of the work, a reprise of the music from the Kyrie. This reprise is one of the most conservative features of the mass, common in mass settings of many composers in eighteenth-century Austria, though last used by Haydn in his pastoral mass, the *Missa Sancti Nicolai*. For Beethoven this bow to tradition might well have encouraged the sense of returning full circle to the point of departure that makes the *Pastoral Symphony* unique in the composer's symphonies, while the attainment of tranquillity through the mediating image of the pastoral is common to both works. The same balming image was to recur in the *Missa Solemnis* where the entire 'Dona nobis pacem' is in the pastoral style, interrupted (as foreshadowed in the Mass in C) by two 'war' episodes. Beethoven's heading for that movement, 'Bitte um innern und äussern Frieden' ('Prayer for inner and outer peace') is a title that could equally well be attached to the earlier symphony. This migration of influence between the sacred and the secular was not to be recognized in the nineteenth and twentieth centuries, but given the greater interdependence of genres in Beethoven's time, the familiarity of the pastoral idiom in a sacred context, and the very fact that Beethoven's own title Sinfonia Pastorella pointed to the legacy, it is difficult to avoid the conclusion that the Mass in C played a determining role in the formation of an emotional groundplan for the symphony. As well as the tone of the two compositions, working with the traditional six-movement scheme of the mass may have encouraged Beethoven for the first time in his career to contemplate alternatives to the standard four-movement structure for a symphony.

That the Mass in C acted as a catalyst in the composition of the *Pastoral Symphony* is suggested by the existence of some further sketches written at the same time as the mass, that is the period July to August 1807.[6] Concept sketches for four of the five movements of the symphony are found: the opening melody of the first movement with the heading 'sinfonia pastorella'; the end of the exposition of the first movement (not used in the symphony); a rising tremolando scale marked 'Donner Bassi' (no exact equivalent in the symphony); a transition or, in truth, an abrupt juxtaposition between the syncopated melody of the trio and the beginning of the storm; the main theme of the fifth movement; and very brief ideas for the varied return of the main theme in the finale.[7] Even though there are no sketches for a slow movement here, taken together these concept sketches suggest that Beethoven had already alighted on the broad scheme for a five-movement symphony since it is unlikely that any symphony would have had two scherzos and no slow movement.

Following the first performance of the Mass in C in September 1807 Beethoven's main task was the completion of the Fifth Symphony, already promised to Count Oppersdorff from Oberglogau in Upper Silesia; he had given the composer a down payment of 200 florins. During the winter the A major cello sonata (Op. 69) and a new overture for *Leonore* (No. 1), intended for a production of the opera in Prague that never materialized, were completed. In March 1808 some letters by Beethoven indicate that he had been suffering from a finger infection that affected his ability to work. It is thought that the Fifth Symphony was finished in February, before the onset of the finger infection. The next major project was the *Pastoral Symphony*, uncommissioned but now something that was clearly much more than an impulse. Beethoven prepared a new sketchbook for the purpose, subsequently devoted to extensive musical sketches for all five movements. In turning to the composition of the work Beethoven might well have been encouraged by the many performances of his symphonies that were taking place in the Liebhaber Concerte. The series concluded on 27 March 1808 with a performance in Italian of Haydn's *Creation*, designed as a tribute to the elder statesman of musical life. Beethoven, along with Prince Lobkowitz, Princess Esterházy and Heinrich Collin, queued up to present his compliments to the composer, as is recorded in Balthasar Wigand's well-known aquarelle (Plate 2). Whether Beethoven had already begun his *Pastoral Symphony* or whether one can indulge the notion that the final stimulus was hearing again one of the two greatest contemporary expressions of the pastoral in music cannot be established. Only the most heartless would wish to deny the appropriateness of the coincidence, and such a person is unlikely to enjoy either work.

March 1808 – December 1808: Realization of the vision

The so-called Pastoral Symphony Sketchbook, the one that Beethoven began about March 1808, contains some 130 pages of detailed work on the five

Plate 2.   A performance of Haydn's *Creation* in March 1808.
Miniature by Balthasar Wigand

movements of the symphony.[8] If the random jottings from the Eroica
Sketchbook and the more considered work from the time of the Mass in C
are added, this amounts to one of the most substantial collections of sketches
for a single instrumental work by the composer. The material contains
extensive drafting of melody, rhythm and harmony, as well as many dynamic
markings and indications of orchestration. Further, and to a greater extent
than in any other large-scale work, there are a number of verbal annotations:
thoughts on the expressive nature of the work in general, drafts for the title
of the work and for the headings of the movements, and comments on single
descriptive passages. Some of these annotations found their way into the
finished product, while others were rejected because they were less acceptable
alternatives or because they were unnecessarily specific. These annotations
provide an intriguing insight into Beethoven's artistic outlook in the work.[9]

Sinfonia pastorella (first appearance in DSB Landsberg 12, p. 48). This title
first appears as a heading for the sketch of the opening of the first movement

made at the same time as the Mass in C and represents Beethoven's first and last thoughts on the title; he did, however, have reservations about it, as will be shown later. The reason for this apprehension may be a simple one: the title was not in the least bit original, in fact the least original of many descriptive titles applied by the composer to individual pieces of instrumental music, such as *Sonate pathétique* and *Sinfonia Eroica*. Its immediate associations with a piece of orchestral music played as part of a church service, as in the Hofmann and Beecke symphonies mentioned in the previous chapter, is confirmed by its appearance alongside sketches for a mass. It was surely never Beethoven's intention that the work was to be a church symphony, yet persisting with this title risked creating that impression. A religious impulse, even a specifically Christian one, played a part in the formation of the symphony, but Beethoven must have realized that using this standard title would not convey the aesthetic range as well as the individuality of the work. Re-inventing the term was impractical, so Beethoven considered an alternative before eventually qualifying it.

Sinfonia caracteristica oder Erinnerungen an das Landleben (*Characteristic symphony or remembrances of country life*) (Pastoral Symphony London, p. 2r). This annotation occurs at the foot of the first page of the 1808 sketchbook. It is not necessarily contemporary with the musical sketches on the page, but it is clearly an alternative to Sinfonia Pastorella. It represents a desire to move away from the church associations of the earlier title, with the subtitle revealing the content of the work in an unambiguous way.

The main title, *Sinfonia caracteristica*, was another generic one, as familiar to Beethoven's public as *Sinfonia pastorella*. F. E. Kirby was the first to draw attention to the significance of this annotation, essentially an indication that the work was to explore one 'characteristic', that is a mood or an image: the pastoral.[10] Daniel Gottlob Türk's treatise, *Klavierschule*, first published in 1789 and a work familiar to Beethoven, makes two pertinent observations on this term. First, he offers the general remark that '*Characteristic* pieces are especially those individual pieces in which either the character of a person or some kind of passion, such as love or pride, is expressed.' The more precise Characteristic Symphony is a term that Türk applies to certain operatic overtures such as those to Gluck's *Alceste* and Mozart's *Don Giovanni* that explore the emotion of the following opera: 'This designation would only be fitting for a symphony of this type, if in general the character of the opera to follow were represented in it or if the composer has expressed immediately preceding action in the symphony.'[11] Beethoven never used this title in any of his works, but the three *Leonore* overtures are clearly good examples of the kind of operatic overture Türk had in mind, while the *Sonate pathétique* (Op. 13), the E♭ sonata *Das Lebewohl, Abwesenheit und Wiedersehen* (Op. 81a), the *Eroica Symphony*, the overture to Collin's play *Coriolan* and the F minor *Quartetto Serioso* (Op. 95) are all 'characteristic' works that explore particular moods.

The concept of a work or a single movement exploring a 'characteristic' is a familiar one from a wide range of music history. Baroque movements that offer one *Affekt* and the single mood of many small piano pieces in the nineteenth century are obvious examples, but Beethoven's interest in the term *sinfonia caracteristica* is very much of his time. In 1797 Paul Wranitzky, a violinist at the two court theatres in Vienna and a leading composer of German opera, composed a symphony to celebrate the signing of the Treaty of Campo Formio, *Grande Sinfonie Caractéristique pour la paix avec la République Française*, a four-movement work in C major with trumpets, timpani and percussion that evoked the joy of peace.[12] Beethoven's *Sinfonia caracteristica oder Erinnerungen an das Landleben* would, therefore, have been an easily understood title. It was perhaps this aspect of the commonplace that caused Beethoven to abandon it. The subtitle, however, was a happy choice. It was modifed from the plural *Erinnerungen* to the singular *Erinnerung* to suggest a single vision rather than a number of disparate ones. The word *Erinnerung* is a crucial one, deliberately imprecise, a memory not an account, and poetic in the celebrated sense of Wordsworth's definition of poetry, 'Emotion recollected in tranquillity'. This desire to promote the feeling of well-being associated with country life, rather than merely depicting country life itself, exercised Beethoven greatly and reveals itself in a number of other annotations.

Man überläßt es dem Zuhörer sich selbst die Situationen zu finden (*One leaves it to the listener to discover the situations*) (Pastoral Symphony London, p. 2r).

Auch ohne Beschreibungen wird das Ganze, welches mehr Empfindung als Tongemählde erkennen (*Also without descriptions will the whole be perceived more as feeling than tone painting*) (Pastoral Symphony Landsberg 10, p. 77).

Sinfonia pastorella – wer auch nur je eine Idee vom Landleben erhalten, kann sich ohne viele Überschriften selbst denken, was der Autor [will] (*Pastoral Symphony – who also treasures any idea of country life can discover for himself what the author intends*) (Pastoral Symphony Landsberg 10, p. 107).

Jede Mahlerei nachdem sie in der Instrumentalmusik zu weit getrieben verliehrt

33

(*All tone painting in instrumental music loses its quality if it's pushed too far*) (Pastoral Symphony Landsberg 10, p. 161).

For eight months in 1815–16 the English composer and pianist Charles Neate was resident in Vienna. He became friendly with Beethoven and during the summer months often accompanied him on walks in the countryside around Baden. In later life he was approached by Thayer for his memories.[13]

Neate, in the course of his long life – he was nearly eighty in 1861 when he related these to the author – had never met a man who so enjoyed nature; he took intense delight in flowers, in the clouds, in everything – 'Nature was like food to him, he seemed really to live in it'. Walking in the fields, he would sit down on any green bank that offered a good seat, and give his thoughts free course . . . walking in the fields near Baden, Neate spoke of the 'Pastoral' Symphony and of Beethoven's power of painting pictures in music. Beethoven said: 'I always have a picture in my mind, when I am composing, and work up to it'.

The 'picture' in the case of the *Pastoral Symphony* is not a painting, much less a photograph. The music is sufficiently allusive, so that the listener can discover rather than be told what the 'picture' is. Carl Czerny, who had been a pupil of Beethoven from 1801 to 1803 and knew him for the remainder of his life, wrote that

It is obvious that in many of his finest works Beethoven was inspired by similar visions and images, drawn either from reading, or created by his own excited imagination . . . But he knew that music is not always so freely felt by the listeners when a definitely expressed object has already fettered their imaginations.[14]

Schindler agreed with Czerny's remarks and discussed the exacting dilemma of how much verbal information should be vouchsafed to the listener.[15]

Czerny, who for many years observed the great master, is therefore correct in saying that Beethoven knew very well that music would not always be felt so freely by its listeners if a specific image were to predispose their imaginations. He would certainly have been reluctant to carry out his plan of making explicit the underlying ideas behind his compositions though it does not seem unlikely that he might have overcome his reluctance in the case of certain works or certain movements.

Schindler's account of Beethoven's aesthetic stance did not prevent him from giving more details about the programmatic content of the symphony, that is drawing attention to the *Malerei* rather than the *Empfindung*.[16] Beethoven's worries about striking an appropriate balance between the two reflected a continuing debate about the function and power of music. In opera, oratorio and song the text provided a focus for the listener's response, but what was the subject matter of the increasingly numerous and popular sonatas, quartets and symphonies? In 1766 the Frenchman Fontenelle had asked, in celebrated exasperation, 'Sonata, what are you telling me?' Other authors, such as Johann Jacob Engel, writing in 1780, proclaimed that the secret power of sonatas and other instrumental music was this very indefiniteness, and that to include specific instances of description was to weaken this power:

The musician should always attempt to convey feelings rather than depict their actual causes. He should present the state of mind and body after contemplation of a certain matter, rather than try to depict that matter or event itself.[17]

During the first years of the nineteenth century these issues were often debated with particular reference to Haydn's two oratorios, *The Creation* and *The Seasons*. Beethoven was an avid reader of the journal *Allgemeine musikalische Zeitung*, reacting sensitively to any criticism of his own music. Its pages contain frequent accounts of the two oratorios; they are invariably affectionate, yet when criticism is proffered it is usually of the excessive use of tone painting, especially in *The Seasons*, a criticism which goaded even Haydn to admit that there was too much pictorialism in that work; 'Frenchified trash' he called it. In May 1804, for instance, Beethoven could have read the following of *The Seasons*:

Another factor renders a judgment of the work difficult. For some time, the misuse of musical tone painting, added to the frequent employment thereof by ignorant composers, have placed in a bad light anything that resembles the tone painting of objects, rendering it suspicious.[18]

Given the fundamental part that Haydn's oratorios played in the inception of Beethoven's symphony, the composer's observations on the pitfalls of tone painting are an attempt to rationalize his position in advance of any criticism. Having decided to compose a Pastoral Symphony rather than a pastoral oratorio Beethoven had already greatly reduced the opportunity for descriptive writing; much of the symphony could concern itself with presenting general musical images of the pastoral. But it is difficult to imagine an entire work of forty minutes or so doing only that. From early on, a brook and a storm were part of the conception; clearly Beethoven was as anxious to include such specifically pictorial passages as he was to contain them within a broader image. This combining of the specific and the general presented him with an unprecedented problem. In the *Eroica Symphony*, another *sinfonia caracteristica*, the issue of pictorialism had not arisen; the hero is never shown in an identifiable heroic situation such as a battle, and the only movement that readily conjures up extra-musical associations is the second, the *Marcia funebre*, where the medium and the message are perfectly related.

Viennese musical taste in the first decade of the nineteenth century often descended to descriptive pieces of the most crass kind. In the same month as the special performance of *The Creation*, the time when Beethoven was beginning sustained work on his symphony, a concert was given in the Leopoldstadt Theatre by a certain Herr Mayer. He specialized in vocalizing sound effects, and with a full orchestra performed a Bird Song Symphony by one Ferdinand Fränzel.[19] The flamboyant organist, composer and theorist Abbé Vogler was especially popular, and his concerts included such trite pot-boilers as *Invocation to the sun at midnight in Lapland*, *The Shepherds' Joy interrupted by a thunderstorm* and *The Siege of Jericho*.[20] Equally popular were the concerts presented by the Bohdanowicz family, one of which mingled operatic arias with a vocal symphony (without text) that contained musical illustrations of hens, a cuckoo, a woodpecker, and a bear hunt complete with yelping hounds and yelling hunters.[21]

The Liebhaber Concerte had been formed to elevate the tone of public concert life in Vienna and Beethoven's symphonies formed a substantial part of the repertoire. At the end of the first season for the composer to contemplate writing a symphony that had bird calls, a storm and joyful shepherds was to risk compromising everything that his art had come to represent. Looked at against this background the annotations on the propriety of descriptive music in the sketches of the *Pastoral Symphony* are as much nervous reassurances as they are statements of lofty aesthetic principles.

Apart from the title of the symphony, its subtitle, and general thoughts on tone painting the sketches contain two other types of verbal annotations: draft titles for individual movements and local indications of tone painting. Alongside some sketches for the end of the first movement Beethoven wrote 'Idillenmässig' ('rather idyllic') (Pastoral Symphony Landsburg 10). In the final score the only local instance of word painting to be identified is that of the three birds at the end of the slow movement. Although there are several pages of musical sketches for this passage the names of the birds are never recorded; perhaps Beethoven thought they were obvious enough. On the other hand the equally copious sketches for the fourth movement, the storm, have many annotations, showing an almost childish glee in pictorialism. 'Donner' ('thunder', sometimes abbreviated as 'Donn') appears several times, always with the *tremolo* figure that appears in strings at the very beginning of the movement and intermittently thereafter; 'Blitz' ('lightning') against the off-beat figure that first appears in b. 33; and 'Regen' ('rain') against a descending scale figure that was eventually to become the motif in b. 3. Unlike the three birds, which are a unique moment of magic, labelling the elements of the storm in the score would have been ridiculous. It should be remembered too that the labelling of the individual birds was for the benefit of the players rather than of the audience, encouraging them to imitate particular bird song; as for members of the audience, 'one leaves it to the listener to discover the situations'.

On the other hand, the titles for the individual movements of the symphony were to be given to the listeners as well as to the players. Draft titles occur for all movements except the storm. Those for the first three movements can be taken together.

Scena. Ankunft auf dem Lande. Wirkung auf's gemüth. (*Scene. Arrival in the country. Effect on the soul.*) (Pastoral Symphony Landsberg 10, p. 149).

Scene am Bach. (*Scene by the brook*) (Pastoral Symphony Landsberg 10, p. 149).

Scena. Festliches Zusammensein (*Merry Gathering*) (Pastoral Symphony Landsberg 10, p. 150).

Appearing on successive pages these titles were probably conceived at the same time, hence the word 'scene' for each movement; in the final product only the second movement retains the word. At this earlier stage Beethoven may well have regarded the symphony as a series of self-contained, though complementary scenes, as suggested by the initial use of the plural *Erinnerungen*. In the *Allgemeine musikalische Zeitung* both *The Creation* and *The Seasons* had been described as a collection or a gallery of pictures[22] and the same idea of an assemblage may have been in Beethoven's mind until symphonic thinking took over and the last three movements were run one into another. This meant that the third scene (*Merry Gathering*) was no longer a self-contained picture, and the word scene was dropped from the title. Perhaps the consequent feeling of a whole encouraged the omission of the same word from the first movement too. Moreover, three scenes rather than one might well have prompted unfavourable comparison with one of Abbé Vogler's pictorial works.

It is often said that Beethoven's first musical thoughts were sometimes commonplace but that he had the ability to transform them into something highly individual. A similar process is evident in the title of the first movement. Compared with the final title of the movement – *Erwachen heiterer*

Empfindungen bei der Ankunft auf dem Lande (*Awakening of happy feelings on arrival in the countryside*) – the draft is uninspiringly factual, like a travel agent's itinerary. By placing the effect first and suggesting the sense of gradual, rather than abrupt transformation the title becomes vastly more resonant. The change from 'Festliches' to 'Lustiges' for the third movement is interesting too; the former suggests something rather restrained, if not formal, whereas the latter is carefree and spontaneous, as befits the music.

On a page of music essentially devoted to sketches for the scherzo (Pastoral Symphony Landsberg 10, p. 135) Beethoven writes *Bach in Dornbach* (brook in Dornbach). Dornbach was a village some three to four miles west of Vienna (now in district XVII). Beethoven is known to have composed the symphony in Heiligenstadt, a village three to four miles north of Vienna; the brook in that village, some fifteen minutes' walk from Beethoven's house, has always been celebrated as the one that inspired the slow movement of the *Pastoral Symphony*, and in 1863 a rather severe bust of Beethoven was unveiled on the bank of the stream, becoming a shrine for countless musical pilgrims. This annotation at least offers the possibility that Beethoven had a totally different brook in mind.

Ausdrucks des Danks (*Expression of thanks*) (Pastoral Symphony Landsberg 10, p. 164).

O Herr wir danken dir (*Oh Lord we thank Thee*) (Pastoral Symphony Landsberg 10, p. 164).

Schleifen (*Gliding*) (Pastoral Symphony Landsberg 10, p. 164).

durchaus sanft (*softly throughout*) (Pastoral Symphony Landsberg 10, p. 164).

These four, well-separated annotations occur on a page of sketches devoted to the coda of the finale, marked 'Ende'; the last two are supported by strikingly long slur marks to suggest the feeling of gliding. The first two reveal a distinctly religious element and a sense of collective well-being. In particular, *O Herr wir danken dir* has a touching frankness of utterance that recalls Haydn's favourite *Laus Deo* (appended to most of his autograph scores) and, more particularly, the declamatory statements that open many choruses in *The Creation* and *The Seasons*. Beethoven's expression of thanks is set to an indecipherable melodic line, a moment of verbalization that can be detected in the final version. In the closing pages of the movement the incessant momentum of semiquavers and $\frac{6}{8}$ rhythms stop; the listener is presented with a tranquil variant of the main theme that culminates in a phrase that could easily have been a setting of the text, 'O Herr, wir danken dir' (Ex. 4).

Example 4

Beethoven was able to devote the entire period from March 1808 through to September to the *Pastoral Symphony*, briefly interrupted by two concert commitments. On 13 April he directed a concert at the Burgtheater for the benefit of the Wohlthätigkeitsanstalten that included performances of the Fourth Symphony, the Third Piano Concerto (with Friedrich Stein as the soloist) and *Coriolan*. At some time in May a concert in the Augarten included the first performance of the Triple Concerto; it is not known whether the composer played the piano but he must have attended. In the summer Beethoven rented accommodation in a favourite village, Heiligenstadt, at 8 Kirchengasse (now 64 Grinzingerstrasse). It is not known when he moved; it could have been as early as May or, more likely to accord with usual Viennese practice, as late as the end of June/beginning of July.

On 8 June, Beethoven wrote a letter to Breitkopf and Härtel in Leipzig, reviving a relationship that had lain dormant for eighteen months.[23]

The tutor of the young Count Schönfeld is the reason for this letter; for he assures me that you would like to have some of my works – Although, since our relations have been broken off so frequently, I am almost convinced that this resumption which I am proposing will again lead to nothing, still I am offering you at the moment, let us say, the following works – two symphonies, a Mass and a sonata for pianoforte and violoncello (let my haste excuse the *ink-blot*) – Please note that I am asking 900 gulden for the whole lot; but this sum of 900 gulden must be paid according to *Viennese currency in assimilated coinage*, details of which must be specially mentioned, particularly in the bills of exchange – In the case of the two symphonies I must for several reasons make the condition that they shall not be published for six months counting from June 1st – I shall probably undertake a journey at the beginning of the winter and should like them, therefore, to be as yet unknown, during the summer at any rate.

The works in question were the C minor symphony, the *Pastoral Symphony*, the Mass in C and the A major cello sonata. The C minor symphony had been completed earlier in the year but it is doubtful whether the *Pastoral Symphony* was finished by 8 June; nevertheless it was sufficiently well advanced for Beethoven to include it in the package. Although Breitkopf and Härtel's reply is not extant it is evident from Beethoven's subsequent letters to the firm, written over the next few months, that the publisher thought the mass unmarketable (it was still rare for masses to be published) and that the total asking price was too high. The reference to a compromise price in the following letter by Beethoven, written in early July, indicates that Breitkopf and Härtel had probably offered 500 gulden.[24]

Here is my decision in reply to your esteemed letter – and you will certainly see that so far as possible I am willing to meet you half-way – Well, let us deal first of all with the scheme, and then with the why and wherefore – I am giving you the Mass, the two symphonies, the sonata for violoncello and pianoforte and two other pianoforte sonatas or, instead of the latter, perhaps another symphony, all for 700 gulden . . . You see that I am giving more and receiving less – but that is really my limit – You must take the Mass, or else I can't give you the other works for I pay attention not only to what is profitable but also to what brings honour and glory.

Apart from the haggling, the letter mentions 'another symphony', a third, strongly suggesting that the *Pastoral Symphony* was no longer a major pre-occupation and that the composer had moved on to contemplate, however inchoately, the Seventh Symphony. According to one source, Beethoven was already working on an opera on the subject of Shakespeare's *Macbeth*, a libretto proposed by Collin.[25]

By the end of July Beethoven had reached an agreement with Breitkopf and Härtel: the package was to consist of the two complete symphonies, the A major cello sonata and two piano trios (Op. 70), though Beethoven is still contemplating substituting a third symphony; the agreed price was to be 600 gulden; and the Mass in C was to be published without any payment.[26] As was normal practice Beethoven did not send his autograph to the publisher but a manuscript copy, prepared by a professional Viennese copyist previously used by Beethoven named Klumpar. His work, checked by the composer, took until mid-September when the manuscript was delivered to Gottfried Christoph Härtel who was visiting Vienna. For over 170 years this printer's copy (the *Stichvorlage*) was lost until it was discovered in 1985; the title page is in Beethoven's own hand, '6ta Sinfonia Pastorella/da/luigi van Beeth[oven]'.[27]

To return to the first letter to Breitkopf and Härtel, that of 8 June, what is the significance of Beethoven's rather cryptic remarks about not publishing the works for six months from 1 June and the likelihood of 'a journey at the beginning of the winter'? The ban on publication suggests that Beethoven was following the practice whereby someone who had commissioned a work retained sole rights over performance and distribution for a fixed period; thereafter such rights were handed over to the composer.[28] There is the implication, therefore, that someone had paid Beethoven for the two symphonies, that performances sponsored by the commissioners were envisaged 'at the beginning of winter', and that the reference to a journey indicated a venue outside Vienna. In 1988, three years after the discovery of the *Stichvorlage* of the *Pastoral Symphony*, another important discovery was made. In the vast archives of the Lobkowitz family a document was unearthed that showed that Prince Lobkowitz approved payment on 17 October 1808 of a bill submitted by the copyist Klumpar for a substantial symphony in F major by Beethoven. It is possible that Lobkowitz was paying the bill for the *Stichvorlage* for Breitkopf and Härtel.[29] Much more likely, however, is that the bill was for orchestral parts, since it is known that Klumpar provided orchestral parts for the Fifth Symphony for the Lobkowitz family.[30] This limited documentary evidence together with the fact that Prince Lobkowitz had arranged semi-private performances of Beethoven's music on several occasions in previous years strongly suggests that the Fifth Symphony and the *Pastoral Symphony* were first performed on one of the Prince's estates in Bohemia in late October or early November 1808. Nothing is known about Beethoven's diary between mid September and 15 November, when he performed at a charity concert in the Burgtheater; he may well have made the journey first mentioned in June. Appropriately, Prince Lobkowitz was to be the joint dedicatee, with Count Razumovsky, of both works when they were eventually published by Breitkopf and Härtel. The likely performances also explain the allusion to the works in Beethoven's letter of 1 November 1808 to Count Oppersdorff, 'You will probably have formed an unfavourable impression of me. But necessity drove me to hand over to someone else the symphony which I composed for you, and another one as well.' The count had, indeed, paid a deposit for the Fifth; Beethoven, with typically ruthless opportunism, gave it to 'someone else', Prince Lobkowitz, along with 'another one', the *Pastoral Symphony*.[31]

In November, back in Vienna, Beethoven's thoughts turned to public performances of the two new symphonies. He was becoming more and more despondent about the city's musical life. The Liebhaber Concerte were not going to continue and Beethoven's discussions with the management of the Burgtheater and the Theater an der Wien for a concert night, which had been going on for over a year, showed no sign of coming to a satisfactory conclusion. Much earlier in 1808 Beethoven had condemned the musical life of the capital; it was hardly a balanced assessment, but there is no doubting the strength of the composer's views: 'I have already become accustomed to the basest and vilest treatment in Vienna.'[32] Chronic dissatisfaction was inflamed in the autumn when Beethoven received an invitation from the self-styled King of Westphalia, Napoleon's son, Jerome Bonaparte, to become Kapellmeister at his court. Beethoven considered this invitation for several months, actually accepting it in January 1809, before an annuity contract financed by Archduke Rudolph, Prince Lobkowitz and Prince Kinsky induced him to stay in Vienna.

It was in this unsettled atmosphere that Beethoven continued to seek a vacant evening at one ·of the court theatres. Finally, as a result of his participation in the charity concert on 15 November Beethoven was allotted the date of 22 December. The preparation for the concert must have been hurried, aggravated by Beethoven's last-minute decision to compose the Choral Fantasy. In these hectic weeks there is evidence that Beethoven was still worried about how the *Pastoral Symphony* would be perceived. On sketches for the Choral Fantasy, there are some drafts for the title for the work, to be printed on the handbill. His initial thought was the overlong *Pastoral Sinfonie Worin die Empfindungen ausgedrükt sind welche der Genuß des Landes in Menschen hervorbringt* (*Pastoral Symphony in which the feelings that the enjoyment of the country arouses in mankind are expressed*). He then wrote the shorter description *Wobej einige Gefühle des Landlebens geschildert werden* (*in the course of which some sentiments of country life are portrayed*). Next, Beethoven's concern about the descriptive passages resurfaces, prompting the drafting of a different continuation to the main title: *Worin keine Malerej sondern die Emfindungen* [*ausgedrückt sind welche der Genuß des Landes in Menschen hervorbringt*] (*in which not painting but the feelings* [*that the enjoyment of the country arouses in mankind are expressed*]).[33] This clumsy syntax seems to have prompted Beethoven to remember the earlier aphoristic formation *Mehr Ausdruck der Empfindung als Malerei* (*More the expression of feeling than painting*) that appeared on the handbill and the performance parts.[34] The most significant difference between, on the one hand, the handbill and performance parts and, on the other, the final title established for publication, is the title of the finale: *Hirtengesang. Wöhltätige, mit Dank an die Gottheit verbundene Gefühle nach dem Sturm* (*Shepherds' Song. Beneficent feeling after the storm joined with thanks to the deity*). This is a frank acknowledgement of a religious impulse for the finale, one that Beethoven removed when he settled on the final title of *Hirtengesang. Frohe, dankbare Gefühle nach dem Sturm* (*Shepherds' Song. Joyful, grateful feelings after the storm*).

The date of the concert was a difficult one because it clashed with a highlight in the Viennese musical calendar, one of the biannual pair of concerts by the Tonkünstler-Societät held in the Burgtheater. Vienna's leading performers were committed to this event, a performance of Haydn's *Il ritorno di Tobia*; consequently Beethoven had to make do with some of the less able players in Vienna mixed, as was the custom, with amateurs. There are many accounts of the difficult rehearsal and of the way the Choral Fantasy broke down in the performance, but none mentions the *Pastoral Symphony*.[35] Prince Lobkowitz was present, an indication of his general support for Beethoven and his particular association with the Fifth and Sixth Symphonies. One account, by the resident Kapellmeister at the theatre, Ignaz von Seyfried, happens to mention the name of one of the violinists, Anton Wranitsky.[36] He was a member of Prince Lobkowitz's court and it is possible that the parts used for the *Pastoral Symphony* were lent by the court; they now survive in the Gesellschaft der Musikfreunde in Vienna (see Plate 3).[37]

In 1817 Beethoven returned briefly to the *Pastoral Symphony*. He had become persuaded of the utility of applying metronome markings to his music, though various comments make it clear that he was well aware of their limitations too. A pamphlet was issued in Vienna by the publishing firm of Steiner that provided metronome marks for the eight symphonies so far completed plus the Septet. Those for the symphonies were printed, without any kind of introduction or commentary, in the *Allgemeine musikalische Zeitung* of 17 December 1817.[38] Although the marking for the first movement is very brisk ($\downarrow$ = 66) and that for the fourth movement ($\downarrow$ = 80) may seem a little measured to some, they are all practicable.

Reaction and publication

The first report of the concert of December 1808 was a brief one in the Viennese journal *Der Sammler* on 5 January 1809.[39]

Plate 3.   Portion of the title page of a first violin part used in the first performance of the *Pastoral Symphony* (Gesellschaft der Musikfreunde, Vienna)

The last days of Christmas week and Christmas day itself were, as usual, dedicated to musical academies. On the 22nd and 23rd of December the local Society of Musicians presented for the benefit of widows and orphans an older oratorio of the immortal Joseph Haydn, Davide penitente [recte: *Il ritorno di Tobia*], performed in the Burgtheater by more than 200 musicians. On the 22nd Herr von Beethoven organized a concert for his benefit in the Theater an der Wien in which he presented to the public the youngest offspring of his inexhaustible talents. All the pieces were by him. Unsurpassedly beautiful was the description of a storm in the first, *Pastoral Symphony*, likewise the Gloria and Sanctus of a mass, which every amateur and connoisseur longingly and fully expected. His imperial majesty the Archduke Rudolph honoured this concert with his presence.

Beethoven was already concerned with supervising the publication of the *Pastoral Symphony*. On 7 January he wrote to Breitkopf and Härtel, requesting that publication should be delayed until Easter because he proposed travelling to Leipzig during Lent, where he hoped to correct proofs and, possibly, direct a performance of the work. He also refers to the concert on 22 December, revealing his concern about his wider reputation.[40]

In spite of the fact that various mistakes were made, which I could not prevent, the public nevertheless applauded the whole performance with enthusiasm – Yet scribblers in Vienna will certainly not fail to send again to the Musikalische Zeitung some wretched stuff directed against me.

Beethoven's paranoia was not borne out by events. On 25 January 1809 the *Allgemeine musikalische Zeitung* contained a report that listed the content of the concert, but offered no evaluation of the works, the author remarking that this could not be done on the basis of one performance and would best be postponed until the printed scores appeared.[41]

Beethoven himself was still undecided about which number to allot the *Pastoral Symphony*. In the manuscript score he had sent Breitkopf and Härtel in September 1808 the work was labelled No. 6; on the handbill for the first performance on 22 December the work was referred to as No. 5. In a letter to Breitkopf and Härtel on 4 March 1809 Beethoven indicated that the order should be the C minor followed by the F major, though his suggested opus numbers of 60 and 61 had already been used for the Fourth Symphony and the Violin Concerto.[42] At the end of the month, even though the plates had been engraved, Beethoven requested corrections and changes. Breitkopf and Härtel asked Beethoven's permission to print the title page in French, the publisher's usual practice, and the printed parts became available to the public in May 1809.

Beethoven's proposed journey to Leipzig had not materialized but a performance of the *Pastoral Symphony* in the Gewandhaus prompted a lengthy evulation of the work in the *Allgemeine musikalische Zeitung*; the critic seems to have had access to the printed parts in advance of publication and at a stage when the publisher was still referring to the work as No. 5. While the writer's general remarks on tone painting reflected well Beethoven's preoccupations, the comment about the indifferent impact of the first movement and the suggestion that the work be termed a fantasy rather than a symphony would have caused deep offence. Most notable, however, are the direct comparisons the critic makes between the *Pastoral Symphony* and Haydn's oratorio *The Seasons*. A couple of months later the *Allgemeine musikalische Zeitung* was to note the death of Joseph Haydn.[43]

A second big new symphony by the same composer (No. 5), likewise just published by Breitkopf and Härtel in accordance with his manuscript and named rural (Pastorale) by the composer himself, is a scarcely less remarkable and individual product. It opens with a fairly simple, good natured Pastorale (Allegro, ma non molto), to which the composer has added the inscription 'Awakening of happy feelings on arrival in the country'; it is certainly not lacking in original touches, although its content is such that the main effect of the symphony inevitably rests on the later movements. There follows an Andante con moto, more precisely designated by the composer as 'Scene by the Brook' – which, in accordance with its idea, is written very simply, with gentleness of feeling and execution, and (clearly quite intentionally) without much variety. It seems to us to be somewhat too long for what it is and what it should be. But the pictorial construction of the whole is ingenious: and even a few incidental imitations of certain little natural manifestations (especially towards the end), treated jokingly, can only be received with a benign smile even by those who otherwise dislike that kind of thing, because they are so aptly portrayed and, as previously stated, only introduced jokingly. The Allegro, No. 3, 'Merrymaking of the Peasants', interrupted by 'Storm and Thunder', Allegro, No. 4, we regard as the most outstanding movements. They are just as they should be, with such novelty and richness of ideas, and such power and effectiveness in their execution that one cannot listen to them without admiration and delight. The bright and quite characteristic merriment in the first of these movements has its counterpart in the rejoicing of the vineyard workers in Haydn's *The Seasons*; the raging storm, with all that accompanies it, is carried through with such energy and tenacity – and without any recourse to the devices usually employed for this purpose – that one truly has to marvel at the master's richness and art. Incidentally, we would not care to attempt to justify all the harmonies that occur here and in several other places during the work. The symphony is fittingly and appropriately completed by an Allegretto ('Shepherds' Song. Happy and thankful feelings after the storm'), although the preceding scenes have a somewhat detrimental effect on this last movement in itself. Haydn was more felicitous in his evening scene after the storm (in *The Seasons*); and so would Beethoven have been if, like Haydn, he had made this last movement even simpler, quieter, and more naive. The whole work is sure to meet with much approval everywhere, as long as one enters cheerfully and with goodwill into the spirit of the author's intentions, without a preconceived opinion. To this end, a word or two, a suitable title, could be of help: we would, therefore, like to observe that it might have been better if this composition had been named 'Fantasia of a composer upon the subject named by Beethoven' rather than a symphony.

4

Design and orchestration

Of Beethoven's nine symphonies the *Pastoral Symphony* was to remain the most original in design: a work in five movements rather than the four that satisfied the composer in his other symphonies. In the last decade of his life Beethoven regularly explored alternative designs for sonatas and quartets but at the time of its composition the *Pastoral Symphony* was a bold step away from the norm of a symphony in four movements. Thirty years or so earlier, when Haydn was composing his 'Farewell' symphony (which could be construed as being in five movements) as well as symphonies in three and six movements, the design of the *Pastoral Symphony* would not have been thought abnormal, but Haydn and Mozart had done so much to affirm the primacy of a four-movement design in the last quarter of the eighteenth century – a trend found in the symphonies of lesser composers too – that this five-movement scheme must have seemed decidedly novel. Such was the appeal of the traditional design of fast, slow, dance movement and finale that it remained the favourite pattern until Mahler; of the major symphonists of the nineteenth century only Berlioz used a five-movement scheme in his *Symphonie Fantastique*, not in emulation of the *Pastoral Symphony* (though distinct influences are apparent), but because for Berlioz tradition mattered little, each work being created *sui generis*.

 Although a five-movement work with titles might have encouraged some of Beethoven's public to approach it as if it were a rag-bag piece by Abbé Vogler such as *The Siege of Jericho*, it is obvious that the design is superimposed on the normal four-movement concept: an opening sonata form movement in a fast tempo, followed by a lyrical slow movement, then two scherzos rather than one, and a finale. The known compositional history of the work offers no evidence that Beethoven ever regarded the scherzo movements as alternatives; all the sketches from 1807 onwards point clearly to a five-movement design while extant ones from before this time offer no guide to the design of the work. Nevertheless, he must have considered how this five-movement approach was going to achieve the same sense of coherence and inevitability found in his previous symphonies. For this reason it is worth pondering what kind of work the *Pastoral Symphony* might have been had one of the scherzo movements been omitted. Of the two movements, *Lustiges Zusammensein der Landleute* and *Gewitter, Sturm*, it is obviously the latter that offers the greater contrast: F minor rather than major, blatantly pictorial and dramatic, a genre piece to vie with storm movements by Haydn, Abbé Vogler and others, and potentially the movement that would most undermine the integrity of the symphony as a whole. Some of the earliest ideas for this movement in the 1808 sketchbook consist of a single *tremolo* D♭ in the bass register, the darkening of the sky before the onset of rain and the full might of the storm.[1] To have followed a self-contained slow movement with the storm would have been an abrupt contrast and might have encouraged an unflattering view of the movement as a mere genre piece. The *Lustiges Zusammensein*, on the other hand, has the advantage of not being a genre piece (except in the sense that the hushed beginning and the one-in-a-bar tempo are general features of Beethoven's scherzo style), but it does not offer the same bold contrast as the storm and would have diminished the impact of the *Hirtengesang*. To a certain extent a storm was *de rigeur* in any work dealing with the countryside; allowing it to exercise its appeal within the framework of a symphony must have been a fundamental concern. Having taken the decision to include a storm, it was almost inevitable that the work would expand to five movements. The *Lustiges Zusammensein* provides an intermediate stage between the complete calm of the *Scene am Bach* and the sublime power of the storm. The allegro tempo, the alternations of two sections (main section and trio section), the contrasting dynamics (from *dolce* and *pianissimo* to *fortissimo* and *sforzando*), the mixolydian tendencies of the opening of the trio, the mixture of *legato* and *staccato*, even the dislocated entries of the solo oboe, all contribute to an increasingly volatile atmosphere. Musically, therefore, the storm arises naturally from the previous movement. On a programmatic level it introduces human beings for the first time, enabling them to be terrified in the storm before being uplifted in the *Hirtengesang*. The end of the storm, too, is carefully controlled so that it, in turn, leads inevitably to the next movement, the *Hirtengesang*. In the Fifth Symphony, the scherzo moves with memorable effect into the finale. In the *Pastoral Symphony* three movements rather than two are linked, providing an equally strong sense of a broad and compelling journey.

At the beginning of the design (summarized below) there are two large, self-contained movements, the first the most deliberately undramatic use of sonata form in an allegro tempo in the whole of Beethoven's output and the second, again in sonata form, creating an even more relaxed atmosphere with its slow tempo and endless lyricism.

I	II	III → →	IV→ →	V
Allegro	Andante molto moto	Allegro – Presto	Allegro	Allegretto
F major $\frac{2}{4}$	B♭ major $\frac{12}{8}$	F major $\frac{3}{4}$ and $\frac{2}{4}$	F minor C	F major $\frac{6}{8}$

The overall key structure helps the broad pattern of tranquillity – disturbance – tranquillity. The F major of the first movement is followed by a fall of a fifth down to B♭ for the slow movement. More unorthodox, and probably unique, is that both these sonata form movements avoid establishing or even merely hinting at a minor key. Both movements rely heavily on the traditional polarity of tonic and dominant at the traditional stages within the exposition and between the development and the recapitulation, while the development sections themselves feature major keys that are a considerable distance from the tonic: D major, G major, E major and A major in the first movement; G major and G♭ major in the slow movement. The third movement again avoids the sound of the minor. After nearly thirty minutes of major key the F minor of the storm makes maximum impact, the discovery of darkness akin to Haydn's discovery of light at the beginning of *The Creation*. Although D♭ major plays an important role in the storm most of the modulations are to minor keys, D minor, G minor, C minor and B♭ minor, the opposite sound world to that of the first three movements. The storm subsides and the music moves comfortingly back to F major and related major keys; not surprisingly, the *Hirtengesang* too eschews minor tonalities, with structural modulations to C major, B♭ major and E♭ major.

This simple opposition of major and minor keys, representing the feeling or, to use Beethoven's word, the *Empfindung* of security and calm, on the one hand, and of disturbance, on the other, is fundamental to the broad impact of the symphony and is without parallel in Beethoven's instrumental output. The location of the minor key as the penultimate stage in the action and as something that is overcome is quite different from the minor-to-major journey for which the composer has always been celebrated, as well as the much more common pattern of a work in the major key turning to the tonic minor in its slow movement and/or trio section of the dance movement. There are, however, some precedents that may have figured in Beethoven's mind.

The part that the Mass in C played in the conception of the *Pastoral Symphony* was noted in the last chapter. Settings of the mass in the Classical period often turn to the minor at the beginning of the Agnus Dei, returning to the tonic major for 'Dona nobis pacem', a characteristic Beethoven was happy to follow in his Mass in C. The transition from the *de profundis* cries of the Agnus Dei to the assured 'Dona nobis pacem' occurs at the same juncture in the *Pastoral Symphony*. In non-programmatic music there are precedents for this strategic placing of the minor key towards the end of the work in two of Haydn's late quartets. The Op. 76 quartets, published by Artaria in July 1799, contain two works, No. 1 in G and No. 3 in C ('Emperor'), whose sonata form finales begin in the totally unexpected key of the tonic minor, turning to the major in the recapitulation section. In the G major quartet, in particular, the minor key provokes a range of modulation and an intensity of mood that are unprecedented in the work. But, whereas in the Classical mass the Agnus Dei is never the only passage in a minor key and the two Haydn quartets include other minor keys before this penultimate stage, in the *Pastoral Symphony* Beethoven presents the contrast at its most fundamental, avoiding any minor keys before this point.

On the basis of seminal works like the Fifth and Ninth symphonies nineteenth- and twentieth-century commentators have often managed to imply that the process of moving from despair (minor key) to triumph (major key) is a pervasive one in Beethoven's output. In fact works that follow precisely this plan are few in number and to will this allegedly favourite plan onto other works should be resisted. The *Pastoral Symphony* is one work that has suffered from this simplistic view of Beethoven's genius. The last movement is not the outcome of struggle; neither is it a transformation. After all it marks the return of F major and the discovery that the listener has travelled full circle to the point of departure, not to a previously unknown, or unknowable destination. Even in otherwise sympathetic performances conductors frequently want to inject the last movement – Beethoven does not use the word finale – with a delirious intensity more appropriate to the Fifth, Seventh and Ninth symphonies. Pastoral subject matter, by tradition, requires a return to normality: Arcadia, not a glimpse of Elysium.

Evoking a journey in the timeless present rather than towards a visionary future is suggested by the fact that the symphony easily embraces the three unities of action, time and place. In all the changes of wording to the title of the first movement Beethoven preserved the word *Ankunft* (arrival); the idea of having left somewhere (by implication the city) was clearly important. The other movements follow on chronologically: by the stream; at a social gathering, by definition in or at a building (Schindler was to say an inn); a storm (in late afternoon?); and after the storm (early evening, as suggested in the review in the *Allgemeine musikalische Zeitung* cited earlier?).

It is worth pondering why the symphony was cast in F major and not in another key. Apart from the early concept sketches for the *Scene am Bach* and the trio of the scherzo all the extant sketches for the symphony are in their due key. Beethoven occasionally voiced his views about the particular qualities of certain keys, calling B minor a dark key and allegedly associating Db major with the pompous Klopstock. Associations of this kind were common in the eighteenth and nineteenth centuries though there was never much unanimity about the precise qualities of individual keys. Sometimes eighteenth-century writers had described F major in terms that seem appropriate to the *Pastoral Symphony*: Kirnberger thought it suited to a 'hunting piece'; Abbé Vogler termed it as 'Silent, lonely' and 'Dead calm' at various times in his life; Schubart thought the key induced 'complaisance and calm'; and Knecht (the composer of *Le portrait musical de la nature*) characterized it as 'gentle and calm'. Other writers, however, saw different attributes or were undecided: Galeazzi described F major as 'majestic' and 'shrill, but not piercing' while Grétry could only manage the feeble comment 'mixed'.[2] Had Beethoven done the unlikely exercise of ascertaining which key was most likely to be associated with pastoral subject matter he would probably have concluded G major; it was the favourite key for pastoral masses and pastorellas, and Abbé Vogler, Schubart and Knecht all ascribed rustic characteristics to the key.[3]

If the general historical background offers little evidence that F major was widely regarded as a pastoral key then the immediate influence of Haydn's two oratorios, *The Creation* and *The Seasons*, is more encouraging; five movements in F major with a more or less explicit pastoral content as opposed to three in G major. For Beethoven himself, following the composition of the symphony there is some evidence that he retained the association of F major with the pastoral. In 1815 he sketched ideas for some projected operas entitled *Bacchus* and *Romulus und Remus*; on one sketch (for which opera it is not clear) Beethoven remarked that 'Throughout the subject must be treated in a pastoral manner', an annotation that is followed by two-and-a-half bars of music in F major.[4]

Casting the symphony in F major did, however, predetermine the orchestral sonority, ensuring a work that was quite different in this respect from Beethoven's previous symphonies. Symphonies Nos. 1 to 5 had all been in keys associated strongly with public performance: C major, D major, Eb major, Bb major, and C minor to C major. They all had the full complement of double woodwind and two horns (three in the *Eroica Symphony*) plus two trumpets and timpani (trombones too in the Fifth). But trumpets in F were hardly ever used and F major, consequently, never had the same impact as C major, D major, Eb major and Bb major; it is largely for this reason that none of Haydn's twelve London symphonies is in F major. In a work that is suffused with tradition the orchestral sonority of the first movement of the *Pastoral*

51

Symphony – strings, woodwind and horns – looks back to the eighteenth century to works such as Haydn's Symphonies Nos. 67, 79 and 89, and Mozart's Symphony No. 18 (K. 130) and the motet 'Exsultate, jubilate' (K. 165). (Ironically, Beethoven's Eighth Symphony, a work often characterized as retrospective, is more forward looking in this respect, requiring trumpets and timpani in its outer movements.)

Starting from this basic orchestra of double woodwind, horns and strings, the smallest in any Beethoven symphony, the composer adds and subtracts other instruments with great delicacy to help shape the drama and narrative of the work, in a way that is common in eighteenth- and early-nineteenth-century opera but without equal in a symphony (see Table 2). When composers needed the sound of trumpets and timpani in the key of F major, as in the slow movements of Mozart's 'Linz' symphony, Haydn's Symphony No. 97 and Beethoven's First Symphony, they usually resorted to using trumpets in C. The third and fifth movements of the *Pastoral Symphony* do likewise. For the storm in F minor, however, Beethoven, stipulates trumpets in E♭ rather than C, because the rich harmonic vocabulary of this movement fits better with the notes available on an E♭ trumpet. Timpani are used only in the fourth movement, so that they are exclusively associated with the stroke of lightning and the roll of thunder. The piccolo is used even more sparingly. Entering in b. 82 of the storm it has only sixteen notes to play, its sustained squealing suggesting the whistling of the wind. Trombones are the last new instruments to enter in the work, strategically placed to mark the height of

Table 2. Wind and percussion instruments in the *Pastoral Symphony*

I	II	III	IV	V
2 flutes	2 flutes	2 flutes	1 piccolo	2 flutes
2 oboes	2 oboes	2 oboes	2 flutes	2 oboes
2 clarinets	2 clarinets	2 clarinets	2 oboes	2 clarinets
2 bassoons	2 bassoons	2 bassoons	2 clarinets	2 bassoons
2 horns	2 horns	2 horns	2 bassoons	2 horns
——	——	2 trumpets	2 horns	2 trumpets
Total 10	Total 10	——	2 trumpets	2 trombones
		Total 12	2 trombones	——
			timpani	Total 14
			——	
			Total 16	

the storm, the diminished seventh that occurs on the last beat of b. 106 (not the natural first beat that characterizes most of the phrase rhythms in the symphony). Unlike the piccolo and timpani, the trombones are retained for the finale, adding a fullness to the middle of the texture that distinguishes this movement from the first. Church music in eighteenth- and early nineteenth-century Austria often used trombones to double the alto and tenor lines (sometimes the bass too), providing the same inner strength. It is often remarked that the inclusion of trombones in this symphony, as in the Fifth, reveals another traditional association, that of the theatre; perhaps in this finale, which at its first performance still had the clause 'thanks to the Deity' in its title, the associations were more religious than secular.

The symphony ends with the magical sound of a muted solo horn, an exceptional tone quality in the music of Beethoven's time. Travelling virtuosos such as the Viennese brothers Anton and Ignaz Böck had been using mutes for thirty years, and their concerts often included gimmicky horn duets with echo effects. The impact of these performances and of the solo at the end of the *Pastoral Symphony* can be gauged from the following passage in Gerber's *Historisch-biographisches Lexikon der Tonkünstler*.[5]

Still more remarkable, evidently, is the new kind of mute which the Viennese brothers Boeck used on their tour in 1783. This device makes the tone sound as though it were coming from a distance several paces away.

5

Technique and image

I Erwachen heiterer Empfindungen bei der Ankunft auf dem Lande
Awakening of happy feelings on arrival in the countryside
Allegro ma non troppo ($\quad= 66$), F major, $\frac{2}{4}$

The paradox of this movement is neatly suggested by its title: the soothing
effect of the countryside encourages a mild excitement. This is not the torpor
of Debussy's faun in the afternoon sun or, more historically relevant, Lucas
in the midday sun in *The Seasons*, but a mixture of anticipation, freshness and
animation. Given the enormous energy and drive that Beethoven had
demonstrated in the opening sonata forms of his first five symphonies, the task
here is radically different. At no point in the compositional history of the work
does Beethoven seem to have considered an alternative to the traditional sonata
first movement, as he did in many piano sonatas of the time; he clearly wished
to retain the procedure of sonata form while controlling its dynamism so that
it became an apt metaphor for the subject matter. The countryside certainly
provided the stimulus, but the absorbing challenge for Beethoven was a
musical one, and as he discovered the technical means so he was able to refine
the title of the movement to match the delicacy of his achievement. The
opening bars of the movement reveal many of the techniques that ensure this
careful mix of animation and relaxation (Ex. 5).

The *piano* beginning to a public symphony is as unexpected as the piano
beginning to the G major concerto played in the same concert. The first four
bars culminate in a pause, to allow the listener to take stock. In Haydn's
Creation, the pause had frequently been used to encourage the listener towards
contemplation and awe, as the natural world stands still in its perfection. It
would have been easy for Beethoven to have appropriated this simple
technique and to have used it extensively; in fact, this is the only pause mark
(apart from the last chord) in the entire movement. Beethoven does not need

Example 5

to halt the flow of the music after this pause because his manipulation of harmonic rhythm makes it unnecessary. The pause in Ex. 5 coincides with the first change of chord in the movement and after this point Beethoven relies on returning the music to a slow harmonic rhythm to achieve the same sense of stasis. Manipulation of harmonic rhythm is a major determinant of the ebb and flow of music in the Classical and Romantic periods and its control was second nature to all practised composers, but in the first movement of the *Pastoral Symphony* there is a particular awareness of the effect of returning the music to a slow rate of harmonic change that in large part explains the character of the movement. The quickening that occurs in bb. 10–11 and again in bb. 14–15 is followed by a passage that sits on the same chord (C major) for ten complete bars, a denial of any forward movement.

In contrast to the slow harmonic rhythm the surface rhythms in Ex. 5 are very active, and it is this conflict that produces the essential quality of excited contentment that was Beethoven's aim in this movement. Of the surface rhythms, the figure ♩♫ ♫♩ ('x') is the most important. To label it a motif would be to suggest the familiar Beethoven process of development, argument and transformation. This particular motif hardly ever promotes new consequences; it is merely repeated.

The natural dynamic base of the movement is *piano*. The movement begins and ends on this dynamic level and most paragraphs within the movement also begin and/or end *piano* too. Although the crescendo beginning in b. 9 that wells up to *forte* in b. 11 represents an appropriate warming of the spirit, short crescendo passages of this type are much rarer than long drawn-out crescendo passages. The ten bars that simply sit on a C major chord are shaped by four bars of crescendo up to the apex of *forte* in b. 20 (marked by the entry of two bassoons) and are followed by a drawn-out decrescendo over five bars to *pianissimo*. In the complete absence of harmonic change, such use of dynamics helps shape many of the paragraphs in the movement. The gentle nudge on the second quaver of the first bar of Ex. 5 is the nearest the music gets to aggression. There is no syncopation in the music, no off-beat *sforzando* accents, indeed very few on-beat accents, no sudden contrasts of *piano* and *forte* or, a speciality from the First Symphony onwards, sudden lunges from *forte* to *fortissimo*. Also absent from this opening and from much of the movement is the automatic accompaniment of repeated quavers. The held pedal Fs and from b. 16 repeated Cs are, as many people have noted, traditional fingerprints of the pastoral. Yet Beethoven avoids overloading the music with pastoral clichés, a discretion that is born of his desire to avoid

Malerei in favour of *Empfindung*, especially at the beginning of the work. The pedal points and the sustained fifths are sufficiently strong allusions to the traditional subject matter.

Ex. 5 has three chords only, F major (I), C major (V) and B♭ major (IV). Arnold Schoenberg is only one of many commentators to have noted the severely restricted harmonic language of this movement.[1] With a handful of exceptions, that are statistically insignificant but musically revealing, the harmonic vocabulary of the movement consists entirely of these three chords, chords moreover that are usually (as in Ex. 5) heard in root position rather than in the more unstable first inversion or, in the case of a dominant seventh, last inversion. Entirely absent from the movement are those chords that colour and control the dynamism of other symphonies, secondary dominants, diminished sevenths, Neapolitan sixths and augmented sixths.

The basic character of the movement, as established by its opening bars, is confirmed by the build up to the first tutti and the tutti itself; the apparent rhythmic energy of this passage is supported by fourteen bars of F major, four bars of C major and seven bars of F major.

The transition section provides the first test of this simplicity of resource. Because the paragraph involves moving from the tonic to the dominant key it cannot, by definition, be as harmonically static as the first subject. Clarinets and bassoons introduce a new triplet figure that contrasts with the duple rhythms of the first subject, a contrast that often becomes a blur in the remainder of the movement. The first violin leads the music to the first and only minor chord in the exposition, D minor (b. 57); emphasized by a *pizzicato* it is sufficiently powerful in this harmonic context to initiate the move to C major. In modern performances (including those on period instruments) this is usually clinched by a hiatus in b. 66 to 'lift' the music onto the dominant of C and the main theme of the second subject area.

While continuing to employ many of the stylistic features of the movement in general – simple harmonic vocabulary, slow harmonic rhythm and long crescendo passages – the second subject introduces two new features, extended *legato* music and dialogue between treble and bass instruments (Ex. 6); had the thematic lead in b. 71 continued upwards in the first violins the result would have been much more forthright. The crescendo that begins in b. 75 reaches a new theme, Ex. 7, which makes extended use of a harmonic texture that was suggested in bb. 13–14 and is to feature especially in the second and fifth movements: harmonic voicing whereby the third of the chord is heard both at the top and the bottom of the texture. A sudden quickening

Example 6

Example 7

of harmonic rhythm to two chords per bar together with a crescendo leads to an excitable version of Ex. 7. The codetta diffuses the situation entirely, resting on C major for twenty-one bars, the rhythms alternating between triplets and duplets, and the melody emphasizing tonic and dominant; the figure is derived from Ex. 7 but is sufficiently close to that of the first subject to lead into it. The whole subsides imperceptibly into *pianissimo*.

This long emphasis on the chord of C major forms a perfectly judged preparation for the repeat of the exposition. It also means that development has to regain harmonic momentum. This it does in thirteen bars of modulation from the dominant of F, through the dominant of B♭, before making a cadence into the key of B♭. The four-bar crescendo to a *forte* (bb. 143–6) seems dangerously abrupt, as does the following *subito piano* and the change of scoring. This points to Beethoven's dilemma. By tradition the development section is an exercise in purposeful musical activity, using material from the exposition to shape new paragraphs. Midway through his career Beethoven was the supreme master of such evolutionary composition, and had even demonstrated in the first movement of the *Eroica Symphony* that the very power of development could threaten coherence and continuity. Had he wished there is no doubt that Beethoven could have used 'x' from Ex. 5 as the building block for a highly intricate development section; it would, however, have been entirely inappropriate. It would have been a denial of the musical properties of the exposition and of the *Erwachen heiterer Empfindungen*. The section develops only in the sense that it further explores characteristics already well established. In proportion the development with 141 bars matches the size of the exposition (138 bars) and recapitulation without the coda (135 bars); its content, however, is more leisurely than either section.

It is in three clear stages, the first beginning at the cadence point in b. 151. Philip Gossett has drawn attention to the importance of the subdominant in the movement as a whole.[2] The second and third notes of the first subject (see Ex. 5) suggest this possibility, the harmonic movement in b. 5 and b. 7 inflects the subdominant and the subsequent crescendo passage leads to a *forte* subdominant chord (b. 11); likewise the recurring refrain of the second subject (see Ex. 7) always ends on the subdominant of C. The fall down to the subdominant to begin the first stage of the development merely emphasizes this process. It initiates the longest crescendo passage in the movement up to this point, twenty-five bars in all from *piano* to *fortissimo*. The thematic material is 'x' from the first subject repeated in each bar but with the rhythms masked by accompanying triplets. The paragraph begins in B♭ and ends in D major but there is no modulation, merely a switch half-way through from a root position B♭ chord to a root position D major. (The incessant repetition and the simplicity of the harmonic language are precisely those techniques employed by modern minimalist composers such as Philip Glass and Michael Nyman. How ironic that they should be found in a composer associated with intellectual intensity!)

Rather than being a new and different process the second stage of the development repeats that of the first stage. After a few bars (bb. 191–6) that again could have led to an intricate thematic development, the music cadences into G major for another long crescendo paragraph with the same characteristics, except that the switch of direction is now down a third, from G major to E major. E major is a long way from F major but Beethoven's journey back towards the tonic in the third stage of the development is a leisurely one through the cycle of fifths, E → A → D → G → C → F, a lengthy procession for which there is no equivalent in a symphony, quartet or sonata by Beethoven. The thematic material is taken from bb. 9–12 of the first subject, with the scoring of bassoons, then violas and cellos emphasizing low murky thirds. When the the cycle of fifths reaches G it turns out to be G minor not G major (b. 255), a darkening of tonality emphasized by the equally novel appearances of *sfp*; these encourage the subsequent *fortissimo* passage in C major to emphasize the phrase rhythms with *sforzando* accents. Sketches for this crucial stage of the movement suggest that Beethoven at one point contemplated that this dominant passage should lead into a *fortissimo* recapitulation of the main theme.[3] He rejected the dramatic approach, preferring to defuse the energy of the *fortissimo* passage, so as to allow the first subject to enter not in triumph but in an atmosphere of calm. Instead of moving from the dominant C at the end of the development section immediately into the tonic F for the recapitulation (an extended perfect cadence), Beethoven interpolates a subdominant chord to form the more relaxed plagal cadence. On Beethoven's autograph manuscript the cadence from b. 275 to b. 279 is signalled by a long decrescendo hairpin mark; earlier in the movement Beethoven had always used the word *diminuendo*, rather than the graphic hairpin. Its appearance here draws attention to the need for an impeccably judged fade into the recapitulation.

Beethoven continues to defuse the tension by replacing the pause of the original first subject, which might have been too rhetorical, with seven bars of single-line decoration; when the full string ensemble enters at b. 289 it is with a sense that only now has the movement regained its proper equilibrium. The passage leading to the full tutti (b. 312) is rescored with clarinets and bassoons taking the lead and first violins (later violas, cellos and bassoons) shrouding the whole with triplets. The remainder of the recapitulation follows the same course of events as the exposition. Given that the recapitulation is a gentle process of confirmation rather than dramatic assertion it might be thought that an extensive coda of a hundred bars, approximately one fifth of the movement, would be unnecessary; the movement could have come to a rest with perhaps a short extension of the rocking tonic–dominant material at the end of the recapitulation (bb. 410–14). Like all Beethoven's extended coda sections this one reviews some of the concerns of the movement as a whole; in addition, it highlights others that are to figure later in the symphony. The coda begins in a similar manner to the opening of the development, which yields a brisk *staccato* passage (bb. 422–7) in *forte* with the fastest harmonic rhythm in the entire movement, three or even four chords per bar. This apparent aberration is easily contained, as the music falls back into the customary slow harmonic rhythm. The tonal starting point for this regaining of composure is the same as that which had established the essential quality of the development section, B♭ major. Coda sections habitually emphasize the subdominant but as well as looking back this subdominant looks forward to the slow movement, which is placed in B♭ major. Throughout the first movement there had been an increasing tendency to feature compound rhythms in contradiction to the prevailing $\frac{2}{4}$; from b. 428 to b. 467 the music is effectively in compound time, another anticipation of the *Scene am Bach*. The symphony as whole is to end with a $\frac{6}{8}$ movement and the very last dramatic passage of the work (finale, bb. 219–37) may be heard as an intensification of the descent from the *fortissimo* top C in b. 458 of the first movement.[4] Nine bars of purposeful harmony (containing the only secondary dominants in the movement) lead to an unexpectedly emphatic cadence and an equally unpredictable continuation: clarinet and bassoon lead the music through a particularly bucolic passage with repeated cadences. The thematic material is derived from the previous *legato* passage but the extended wind scoring and the simplistic cadences are a foretaste of passages in the third movement, the *Lustiges Zusammensein der Landleute*. The various cross-references between movements in the Fifth Symphony have often attracted attention. In the very different world of the *Pastoral Symphony* Beethoven shows an equal regard for the integration of movements.

II Szene am Bach
Scene by the brook
Andante molto moto ($\flat.$ = 50), B♭ major, $\frac{12}{8}$

In performance, the slow movement is the longest in the *Pastoral Symphony*, some two minutes longer than the first movement. Indeed it and the *Marcia funebre* of the *Eroica Symphony* are the largest slow movements in Beethoven's nine symphonies, certainly longer than the slow movement of the Ninth. Such cold-blooded statistics point to an expressive truth, that the slow movement of the *Pastoral Symphony* represents country life at its most relaxed; it is not, therefore, a contrast with the first movement, as often in symphonic works, but a natural outcome of it. The movement is a vast, leisurely sonata form in which lyricism and richly imaginative orchestration play a determining role. There are two notable precedents in Beethoven's output, the slow movement of the Septet (Op. 20, 1799) and that of the Second Symphony (Op. 36, 1801–2); both are generous in their melodic appeal (six themes in the Larghetto of the Second Symphony), while the $\frac{9}{8}$ metre and concertante writing of the Septet make it particularly close in spirit. Unfolding a melodic line over a continuous accompaniment is a common texture in slow movements of the eighteenth century, both vocal and instrumental, and it is one that can be traced back to the seventeenth century. Here in the *Pastoral Symphony* it is an appropriate musical metaphor for the endless flow of the brook. But Beethoven's title is 'scene by' the brook, not the brook alone, and the appearance of the nightingale, quail and cuckoo at the end of the movement are pointed indications of this; that they emerge naturally out of the figuration and texture of the movement suggests that the general ambience of which the brook is a part is more important than the brook itself. In recognizing that this is not a comatose *reflets dans l'eau* Beethoven's cautionary 'Mehr Ausdruck der Empfindung als Malerei' should be remembered and the temptation resisted of particularizing the music before the composer is ready to do so. The labelling of the three birds is not a casual indulgence by the composer, much less a hint that there are further literalisms; rather it is an acutely conscious moment in a movement that is otherwise overwhelmingly subliminal in its working.

Nevertheless, the sound world of this movement is highly distinctive, and much less routine than that of the slow movement of the Septet. Two solo cellos, *con sordini*, are detached from the body of the cellos and double basses, and play a separate line for much of the time. Their prime function is to create a texture with a low centre of gravity, plenty of low thirds as foreshadowed in the first movement; elsewhere they share the thematic lead, the two muted cellos providing a subdued quality whereas a full section might have been dangerously rich. Beethoven's autograph and the parts used for the first performance indicate that the violins too are to be muted, an indication that did not survive into the printed score; many modern performances, especially on period instruments, now adhere to the composer's first thoughts.[5] After the first four bars of quavers the accompaniment turns to semiquavers which aid the opaqueness. For the duration of this first subject paragraph (bb. 1–18) the sonority is underpinned by the slow-moving tonic and

Example 8

dominant pitches of the horns. Thematically, the paragraph consists of a melody played by the first violins and repeated by clarinet and bassoon; on the repetition the violins add a trill figure to the accompaniment, part of the process of accrued decoration that occurs throughout the movement. The paragraph ends with a short, but equally lyrical theme (Ex. 8); the hints of overlapping imitation it contains are to be exploited later in the movement.

Like the equivalent paragraph in the first movement the transition (bb. 19–30) begins with a shimmering, repeated note figure. However, unlike the first movement, Beethoven does not then take a direct route to the dominant, but presents a third look at the main theme, its initial, hesitant phrases becoming ever more eloquent as the dominant of F is confirmed; first the resolution of the appoggiatura is lengthened by a crotchet (bb. 23–4) then the appoggiaturas themselves are lengthened (bb. 27–8).

The second subject is initiated by a solo flute, followed by a solo bassoon. Up to this moment, following the example of the first movement, the harmonic language has consisted almost entirely of primary triads, with phrasing patterns clearly articulated by perfect cadences. Beethoven now capitalizes on this simplicity: the first phrase of the flute leads not into F, which would have been very short winded, but to an extension of the dominant chord; at the equivalent point in the bassoon solo the music moves magically onto an A major chord, a change of colour that is repeated in the two subsequent bars. As in the first movement the effect of this change of harmonic colour is dependent on the slow harmonic rhythm and the simplicity of the surrounding language. That these two complementary resources were a major concern of Beethoven in this symphony is suggested by the next cadence (into b. 41). Following a crescendo to a *forte* Beethoven exaggeratedly draws attention to the cadence by changing the compound rhythms to duple rhythms for the cadential $^6_4$ chord followed by a complete bar from which the previous continuous motion is absent, the only continuity being supplied by a cadential trill. Momentum is almost lost, only to be recaptured by the resolution once more onto an A major chord. (On the autograph score this bar of suspended animation (b. 40) is squashed in at the end of a page, suggesting that it was a late addition. But the sketches clearly show that it was always intended,[6] and that the squashed appearance of the autograph was due to a miscalculation in the writing up of the score.) One more repetition of the theme leads to a cadence in F major – again cleverly elongated to remove the energy of the previous crescendo – and the return of Ex. 8. A further four bars (bb. 50–4) integrates the movement even more by referring directly to the opening accompanying figure.

The development section has three clear stages, summarized below.

	STAGE 1	STAGE 2	STAGE 3
Bars	bb. 58–68	bb. 69–78	bb. 79–91
Key	G major	E♭ major	G♭ major→V/B♭
Thematic material	1st subject and cadence theme	1st subject and cadence theme	1st subject
Leading instrument	flute and oboe	clarinet	violin 1

Wholescale repetition is, once more, the hallmark of the section, enhancing the prevailing mood, rather than modifying or contradicting it. The three main paragraphs are each in a major key with an emphasis on modulation to a key that is a third away; rather than the switch of keys that characterized the first movement the concluding bars of Stages 1 and 2 use the cadence theme (Ex. 8) to channel the music towards the new tonal goal. The G♭ major in Stage 3 could have become inappropriately forceful had the journey back to B♭ followed the conventional path of ♭VI→Augmented sixth→V$^6_4$→ V→ I into B♭. Instead Beethoven treats the G♭ chord as the dominant of B major (b. 82), encouraging a less orthodox and, crucially, less purposeful move to the dominant of B♭. Five bars of dominant preparation without a clear melodic content then lead into the recapitulation. Each stage of the development features the first subject led by a different concertante instrument. In the first two stages the leading instruments (oboe and flute, then clarinet) warm to the beauty of the melody, become ever more rhapsodic and conclude with a cadential trill. The ascending G major figure in b. 58 in the flute has prompted discussion and speculation quite out of proportion to its musical function as a decorative arpeggio. It all began with Anton Schindler.

In his biography of Beethoven written in the 1850s Schindler gave a lengthy account of the *Pastoral Symphony* that sought to stress Beethoven's empathy with country life. To this end the author included reminiscences of conversations he allegedly shared with the composer.[7]

Between Heiligenstadt and Grinzing there lies the pleasant, grassy valley of a gently murmuring brook that rushes down from a nearby mountain side. While crossing this valley, overhung here and there by tall elm trees, Beethoven would frequently pause and let his enraptured gaze wander over the spectacular scene before him. Once he sat down on the grass and, leaning against an elm, asked me if there was a yellow-hammer singing in the topmost branches of the trees. But all was quiet. Then he said, 'It was here that I composed the "Scene by the Brook", and the yellow-hammers up there, the quails, the nightingales, and the cuckoos composed along with me.' When I asked him why he had not set the yellow-hammers into the scene, he seized his sketchbook and wrote [the flute figure in b. 58]. 'It is the little lady up there who composed that' he said, 'and does she not have a more important role to play than the others? Those other songs are merely meant for a joke.' And truly, the entrance of this theme in G major [Stage 1] lends the tone-painting more charm. Continuing on the subject of the whole symphony and its parts, Beethoven said that the song of this species of yellow-hammer was very close to the scale he had written down in *andante* tempo and the same pitch. He explained that he had not labelled the yellow-hammer's passage because such a thing would only have added to the great number of malicious interpretations that had already hampered the reception and reputation of the work in Vienna and elsewhere.

The revelation that there was an extra bird in the slow movement produced a rash of comment and speculation at the end of the nineteenth century and the beginning of the twentieth century. Was this figure, covering nearly two octaves, a realistic evocation of a yellowhammer? Were there yet more birds hidden in the movement, such as a woodpecker? Donald Tovey who must have been familiar with this ornitho-musicological speculation had little time for the whole business. He dismissed Schindler as 'Boswell without the genius' and someone who 'bored Beethoven so fearfully with silly questions that Beethoven generally put him off with answers of the same quality'; he mocked the whole business by claiming the call was that of a new unrecorded species, 'the giraffe-throated yellow hammer'.[8]

In 1993 the American scholar Owen Jander returned to the question of Schindler's yellowhammer, revealing the interesting fact that *Goldhammer* had always been mistranslated and that goldfinch was the proper English equivalent; further, that in Venetian dialect the bird is called *gardellino* and in Vivaldi's flute concerto with that title (Op. 10, no. 3, RV 428) the same upward arpeggio is heard.[9] This would seem to suggest that Schindler was not as fanciful as Tovey and many people after him have understandably maintained, and perhaps Beethoven did associate the figure with a *Goldhammer*. Even if Beethoven did make the association – whether to appease the bore Schindler or not is immaterial – the fact remains that it is not indicated on the score, partly because it is a detail of the accompaniment not the principal voice and, more important, because at this stage of the movement it would have been premature to do so; Beethoven is not yet ready to be specific. Putting Schindler's testimony to one side it is worth remembering that the figure arises naturally out of the previous material, the *staccato* semiquavers in the first violins in the preceding four bars, themselves a version of the semiquaver motion that occurs in much of the movement. The solo flute itself makes this connection when its *staccato* arpeggios turn in b. 62 to *legato* arpeggios. In one of the earliest sketches for the slow movement in the 1808 sketchbook the G major arpeggio semiquavers occur notated in the lower reaches of the bass clef,[10] clearly not an aural reminiscence of a particular bird – unless of the steroid-eating, giraffe-throated yellowhammer – but an early indication of a figure that was to become an important detail of the accompaniment.

Given that the development section had featured three verbatim statements of the first subject, it is not surprising that in the recapitulation (beginning in b. 91) the first subject paragraph is shortened; the repetition of the theme is omitted. For this, its fifth and final appearance, the theme is once more differently orchestrated: a full tutti sound but in *piano* dynamic, melody in the flute later joined by first violins, and with the *staccato* arpeggio figure distributed between bassoon, clarinet and first violins. After an interrupted cadence (b. 97) the theme moves on to the second, melodically expansive part of the transition. Thereafter, for the most part, the second subject paragraph retains the same thematic content and scoring as the equivalent section in the exposition.

The beginning of the coda (b. 125) is devastatingly simple, a pair of two-bar phrases, each with a crescendo–diminuendo designed to emphasize the dying fall onto the subdominant. The lack of a strong melodic identity together with the full sonority sets up the following passage. Three solo instruments enter in turn depicting the nightingale, quail and cuckoo; the cadence theme (Ex. 8) makes a brief appearance before the trio returns; finally, the cadence theme leads the music to a close. The melodic depiction of the birds is obvious enough and the listener does not need to be told that it is a passage of tone painting, yet the material emerges unforced from its context of trills, duplet quavers and melodic emphasis on the submediant. Moreover, the instruments themselves are precisely those that had taken concertante roles in the development section; their tendency in that section towards individual display is here formulated into birdsong, a perfect union of music and image. The solo writing and the location of the passage towards the end of the movement suggest a cadenza, but Beethoven belies that association by making the music sit on a static tonic chord in root position, rather than on the customary second inversion.

Many of Beethoven's earliest draft outlines for the movement in the 1808 sketchbook do not have the bird calls at all;[11] one ending is based on quaver motion in fifths and sixths, suggesting soft repeated horn calls; another, marked *Ende*, alternates the same figure with a single bar of trills on the tonic. These trills and the recognition that they occur throughout the movement, as already notated in many pages of sketches, seem to have prompted the decision to include the imitation of birdsong.

The pages of the autograph devoted to the coda show that Beethoven was still dissatisfied at this late stage. There are several layers of working, with innumerable crossings out. One particularly awkward corner for Beethoven was the lead into the return of the birdsong. A reconstruction of the composer's first thoughts on the autograph is given in Ex. 9. The cadence theme is halted after a complete bar; after the silence a dominant chord heralds the return of the birds. This silence was evidently too abrupt, and the preceding cadence is certainly rather lame. In the final version Beethoven halts the cadence theme two beats earlier, with the birdsong entering above a tonic chord; the result is the perfectly judged feeling of bated breath that is so appropriate to this moment of rapt wonder.

III Lustiges Zusammensein der Landleute
Merry gathering of the country people
Allegro ($\downarrow$. = 108), F major, $\frac{3}{4}$

After the repose of the Andante the third movement marks the beginning of the process of disruption. By inclination a scherzo movement can much more easily accommodate the pictorial than can a sonata form first movement and a lyrical slow movement, if only because any scherzo is bound to be *lustig*. But Beethoven's third movement is not a pictorial genre piece. As in the slow movement the obviously graphic moments – the village band sequence led by the off-beat oboe and the peasant dance of the trio section – emerge out of a context that is not specifically pictorial, so that once again the effect is one of *Empfindung* rather than *Malerei*.

Example 9

From about 1800 onwards Beethoven is as likely to leave his scherzo movement without that title as he is to use it; of the nine symphonies only the Second and Third use the word as a heading, though virtually all the movements have stylistic and formal features that can be accommodated by the generic term scherzo. In the *Pastoral Symphony* the broad outline of a main scherzo section (bb. 1–164) enclosing a trio section (bb. 165–204) is obvious, as is the general brisk tempo. To provide the necessary internal balance to match the expanded dimensions of the symphony Beethoven requires the whole of the trio section to be repeated after the reprise of the scherzo, a scheme first encountered in Beethoven's symphonies in No. 4. It has been convincingly argued that Beethoven's original intention in the Fifth Symphony was to have the whole of the scherzo and trio played twice, which when joined with the link into the finale made a five-part design of scherzo – trio – scherzo – trio – link;[12] this is the pattern adopted in the *Pastoral Symphony* too. A final characteristic of the scherzo in the *Pastoral Symphony* that is general rather than particular is the nervous *pianissimo* of the opening; the third movements of the *Eroica Symphony* and the Fifth are further examples.

As well as striking a balance between *Empfindung* and *Malerei* the movement has to effect the transition between the calm of the slow movement and the onset of the storm; it has to generate an unease that makes the storm inevitable. Modulation to keys a third away had been a feature of the development section of the first two movements; here that characteristic is introduced immediately, the first event in the movement, *staccato* F major versus *legato* D major. After the orchestral opulence of the slow movement the sparse octave unison of the third movement is a telling contrast, though the tonic pedal points (bassoons, pointed by cellos and basses) that appear when the music is in D major are a careful reference to the world of the pastoral; during the rest of the movement *legato* phrases are always associated with pedal points and gradually give way to *staccato* crotchets, simple musical equivalents for the calm and the gathering storm. When the *staccato* material is heard above a dominant pedal (b. 41 onwards) it produces the longest *fortissimo* passage in the work up to this point, thirty-four bars, with, moreover, twenty-five successive *sforzando* markings and strongly emphasized cadences. Equally significant in this movement is the absence of controlled diminuendo passages of the kind used in the first movement to uncoil the power of crescendo passages.

The splendidly raucous cadences in bb. 75–83 could easily have marked the end of the scherzo; instead Beethoven moves swiftly into a second stage. In an uncharacteristic desire to pigeon-hole the structure of the music, Tovey, who recognized the potentially self-contained nature of the music up to this point, wanted to term the following wind band passage the trio, undervaluing the essential continuity of the music and, more perversely, the abrupt change of tempo and metre that occurs later at b. 165.

Many scherzo movements by Beethoven play fast and loose with the natural beat of the music. In the *Pastoral Symphony* the inability of the leading lines (oboe, clarinet and, initially, horn too) to begin their solos on the appropriate beat of the bar despite the basic accompaniment provides a sustained *musikalischer Spass*. The solo scoring satirizes inexpert players but also, as anyone who has directed or taken part in shaky amateur music-making will recognize, their uncanny ability to contrive a plausible result. Some commentators have observed that the oboe enters a beat early; in fact, it is two beats late. Taking the two-bar rhythms established with great gusto at the end of the previous tutti as the norm, Ex. 10 recreates what should have happened, an amiably jogging eight-bar phrase. Bassoon and strings cling tenaciously to their parts; the oboe, because it enters late has to readjust the line going into

Example 10

b. 95, prompted by the bassoon. A similar process happens in the following phrases. The clarinet, when it takes the lead, is no better but with the shameless confidence of many a dullard concludes with a virtuoso descending arpeggio. The horn, likewise, begins off the beat but its *legato* phrases restore calm, signalled too by undisturbed phrasing patterns, the *piano* dynamic and a tonic pedal later expanded to an open fifth, in other words a return to the pastoral norm.

Only the most determinedly positivist commentator could give an account of this episode that avoided all extra-musical gloss. For Schindler it was the second passage in the symphony for which he felt able to vouchsafe the true intention of the composer.[13]

The other indication I was given of the composer's intentions concerns the third movement: 'Merrymaking among the Country Folk'. Viennese music-lovers of the time must have guessed the composer's intentions regarding this movement without his explaining them. They apparently recognized in the phrasing of the first part in ¾ time an imitation of Austrian dances, if not a parody of them such as a man like Beethoven would have been capable of writing. At that time there still existed in Austria a typical folk music whose rhythms, harmony, and performance could not have failed to charm even the most highly educated musician . . .
At the inn of 'The Three Ravens' on a marshy meadow near Mödling there had for

many years been a band consisting of seven instrumentalists. It was from this group that the young musician newly arrived from the Rhineland first heard the genuine national music of his new homeland. They became acquainted, and Beethoven immediately composed some sets of Ländler and other dances. In 1819 he once more agreed to a request from this group for new music. I was with him when he handed the new score to the leader of the Mödling band. The master remarked gaily that he had written these dances in such a way that the musicians could take turns laying down their instruments to rest or take a nap. When the visitor had left us, full of joy over the famous composer's gift, Beethoven asked me if I had noticed how village musicians would often fall asleep while playing, sometimes let the instrument sink and not play for a while, then wake up with a start, make a few hearty blasts or bowings at random, yet usually in the right key, and then go back to sleep again. In the *Pastoral Symphony* he had tried to 'copy these poor people'.

Now, dear reader, take the score in hand and see for yourself the 'devices' in pages 106–9. Notice the stereotyped accompaniment in both violins on pages 105ff [from b. 87]; notice further the drowsy second bassoon with its repeated two notes while the contrabass, cello and viola are not heard at all. The viola does not wake up until page 108 [b. 127], then it seems to awaken its neighbour the cello. The second horn emits three blasts, then falls silent again. At last the contrabass and both bassoons rouse themselves with renewed vigour, and the clarinet is allowed to take a break.

Unlike the contentious *Goldhammer* of the slow movement few would want to deny the appropriateness of this commentary, even if Schindler is rather oddly concerned with the accompaniment and not the leading line. But, as always with this author, it is another question whether the account derives from Beethoven. Schindler did not meet Beethoven until 1822 and if indeed the composer had been thinking of sleepy village musicians it may have been an interpretation that occurred to him after the composition, if not, as sceptics will aver, to shut up his inquisitor. Yet the physical appearance of the autograph score suggests that 'the drowsy second bassoon with its repeated two notes' may have stuck in Beethoven's mind. The autograph clearly shows that all the bass entries were originally written in single crotchets on the first beat of the bar; Beethoven changed them to dotted minims, an undeniably more comic effect.

A peripheral issue raised by Schindler's report is that Beethoven composed a set of dances in Mödling in 1819 that allowed the players to catnap in turn. These have not survived, casting doubt, once more, on Schindler's veracity. In 1905 Hugo Riemann discovered a set of dances which he claimed to be the 'lost' Mödling dances (WoO 17), but they do not fit Schindler's description. Taken with the poor status of the source this must mean that they are of doubtful authenticity.[14]

Example 11

A three-bar link propels the music into the trio section, a furious and heavily accented dance. Beethoven had already hinted at its characteristic rhythms in the clarinet solo in the coda of the first movement (b. 476). In the *Ritterballet* from 1790–1 (WoO 1) there is a movement entitled *Deutscher Gesang* whose rhythms and *sforzando* accentuations are almost exactly those of this dance (Ex. 11).[15] There is no need therefore to quibble with Schindler's remarks on the section.[16]

The Allegro on page 110, in $\frac{2}{4}$ time, is inspired too, in form and character, by Austrian dance music of the time. There were dances in which the $\frac{3}{4}$ measure suddenly gave way to a $\frac{2}{4}$ bar. In the 1820s I still used to hear such dances in villages within a few hours' distance of the capital, such as Laab, Kaltenleutgeben, Gaden, and others.

The $\frac{2}{4}$ idea was one of the concept sketches in the Eroica Sketchbook which suggests that it was an aural reminiscence of an actual dance. In the 1808 sketchbook there is an isolated musical detail which was clearly of some significance to Beethoven, a semibreve E with a pause mark falling down a third to C, a figure that sounds like a bugle call or posthorn signal.[17] He was obviously anxious to include this figure, but he lacked an appropriate instrument to evoke it. Up to this point in the movement the composer had utilized two horns in F, natural instruments that could not play the long held E. For that reason Beethoven adds two trumpets in C to the score in the trio; they certainly add to the general clamour when they first enter in b. 181 but their real value is to sound out this call (bb. 203–4, first trumpet). There follows a complete repetition of the whole movement, allowing the contrast of repose and aggression to be experienced once more. The final section is a coda, or rather a link into the Storm. Beginning like a third statement of the opening of the movement, the section goes awry when the answering eight-bar phrase is forced to return to F, rather than being allowed to move to D major. The following thirty bars of unrestrained *fortissimo* are played presto (Beethoven does not a supply a metronome mark for this section); the *Empfindung* is one of uncertainty, even panic. The storm is inevitable.

During the *Lustiges Zusammensein der Landleute* Beethoven has skilfully moved away from the musical language of the first two movements; tempo, rhythm, phrase patterns, dynamics and orchestration are all more volatile as

the calm of the 'remembrance of country life' is disturbed. Disturbance turns to disintegration in the following movement.

IV Gewitter, Sturm
Storm
Allegro ($\downarrow$ = 80), F minor, ₵

The presto repeated cadences of the end of the third movement never reach their destination of a stable F major, but land on a *pianissimo*, *tremolo* D♭ on low strings. The tonic chord is held back until b. 21, when F minor is heard *fortissimo* with, as previously noted, the first timpani roll in the symphony. The isolated prominence given to this D♭ in the sketches symbolizes the disruptive power of this movement within the symphony. Every element of the musical language is now altered fundamentally.

F minor is not merely the negation of the preceding F major, but constitutes the first minor triad of any prominence in the symphony; even the peasants were not allowed to stray towards a sentimental use of the minor key. While F minor is unequivocally the opposite of F major it is not a static F minor, the speed of modulation and the variety of tonal destination being unequalled in any of the previous three movements: six different keys (F minor, B♭ minor, D♭ major, C minor, A major and D major) in the space of just over three minutes. By coincidence a total of six different keys had featured in each of the first two movements, but each of those movements had taken a leisurely ten minutes or more to traverse its tonal territory. Moreover, whereas the earlier movements had cultivated a simple diatonicism, with long stretches of the music sitting on common chords, much of the harmonic weave of the Storm consists of diminished sevenths and chromatic scales.

Cantabile melodic lines or jaunty folksongs are not something one hears in a storm and the thematic content of the music is based instead on a set of short thematic motifs that would defy any singer in their speed, register, range and angularity (Ex. 12, a–h). Dynamics too play a fully disturbing part. Since tense anticipation of the next flash of lightning or stroke of thunder is as much part of the power of a storm as the lightning and thunder themselves, the *pianissimo* passages are as carefully deployed as the *fortissimo* ones. The opening *pianissimo* leads inexorably to the *fortissimo* tutti. From b. 39 the dynamics change more frequently: *sforzando* markings on the beat, sudden *pianissimo*, off-beat *sforzando* (not heard previously in this symphony) and that most unnatural of demands, a crescendo down a chromatic scale.

In comparison with the previous movements the music avoids strongly

Example 12

articulated cadences; the ambitious tonal structure of the movement is dependent on dominant chords moving to their respective tonics, but often with one or both in inversion. The move from the expected cadence in F minor to an A major chord in b. 56 is particularly brutal, a dehumanized version of the repeated interrupted cadences in the slow movement.

For the listener the sweep and power of this movement pose no problems and though Beethoven labelled thematic ideas in the sketches thunder, lightning and rain, they are self-evident without the reader having to make a mental record of them as they pass by. The ease with which the movement is comprehended tends to obscure the fact that its musical language represents Beethoven at his most probing. In third-period Beethoven 'difficult' music is often densely contrapuntal (e.g. the *Grosse Fuge* or the finale of the 'Hammerklavier' sonata) or combines an extremely slow tempo with a highly ornate texture and the simplest of harmonies (e.g. the second movement of the last piano sonata, Op. 111). There would seem to be no parallel for this movement, with its hugely expansive harmonic vocabulary deployed in a brisk tempo. It could be said to be Beethoven's considered reply to Haydn's

Table 3

Bar	1–20	21–33	33–40	41–48	49–55
Key	D♭ maj→	F min→	B♭ min→	D♭ maj→	C min→
Motif	a, b	c	d, e	f, d	f, d
Dynamic	pp, cresc	ff	ff + sf	pp, f, sf, pp	p, cresc, f
Bar	56–61	62–67	68–77	78–88	89–94
Key	A maj→	D maj→	→	C min→	D♭ maj→
Motif	a	f, a, b	a	g	e
Dynamic	p	pp	pp, cresc	ff, sf	ff, sf
Bar	95–118		119–35		136–55
Key	chromatic		B♭ min, C min, D♭ maj→		V/F maj
Motif	h		g		f, d, i
Dynamic	p, cresc, f, ff, sf		ff, dim		pp

'Representation of Chaos'. The shape of the Storm is as much a guide to the conductor and players as it is to the listener, yet the movement lacks the easily perceived form of the first three movements. But the lack of a standard form is not the same thing as formal incoherence. Table 3 plots the course of the movement, summarizing its tonality, thematic content and prevailing dynamic.

As is fundamental to musical language from the mid-eighteenth century onwards a new key coincides with a change of melodic material, often supported by a change of dynamic and (not shown in the table) texture and orchestration too. Using these basic principles Beethoven builds a movement that consists of a series of paragraphs, each around ten bars. Only eight bars are actually in the home tonic of F, the lengthy dominant pedal at the end having to draw together B♭ minor, C minor and D♭ major, as well as the more distant keys of A major and D major. On sketches for the movement Beethoven wrote 'In zwei Theile' ('In two parts').[18] This does not mean binary, though some commentators have viewed the paragraph in C minor beginning at b. 78 as the beginning of the second part of a binary movement. Two, more plausible interpretations suggest themselves. First, it is possible that 'parts' refer to the broad progress of the storm itself: build up and decay. Alternatively, it may indicate the two-fold approach to the full fury of the storm that is apparent in the structure of the movement.

The storm threatens and breaks out in the first three sections, introducing

the thematic elements 'a','b', 'c', 'd' and 'e'; it subsides, going back to D♭ and the dynamic of the opening, even to its motif in the sense that 'f' is an elaboration of the single *tremolo* D♭. The second approach (b. 41 onwards) is more protracted and complex, and consequently more menacing; the sound effects are the same ('a', 'b', 'd' and 'f') but the colour of the sky is now more varied (C minor, A major and D major). The second outburst of the storm is in C minor and D♭ major, and the apex of the storm is the totally chromatic section beginning in b. 95. The subsiding of the storm sees the return of B♭ minor, C minor and, most significantly, D♭ major, the most frequently encountered key in the movement; it had been the source of the harmonic disturbance and had twice presaged a new intensity. From b. 126 its power is distilled gradually onto the dominant of F major. The dominant preparation that occupies the remaining twenty bars continues into the beginning of the fifth movement and finally resolves when the main theme of the finale is announced (b. 9). As well as the home key of F major the entire musical language of the first two movements is to be regained; it would have been quite inappropriate for the dominant pedal to have led to a triumphant *fortissimo*. The whole process is exquisitely paced. A few remnants of the storm remain (motifs 'f' and 'd', together with diminished seventh harmonies) but gradually the old musical language emerges: soft dynamics, consonant harmonies and longer note values. A new hymn-like melody is heard ('i') with, on its second appearance, the distinctive low thirds of the first two movements. George Grove was the first to point out that this melody is an augmentation of motif 'a';[19] likewise, the flute scale that leads into the fifth movement may be heard as a transformation of motif 'f'.

With this flute scale the symphony returns full circle to the quietude of the first movement. In Handel's *Acis and Galatea* Arcadia is returned to its former tranquillity after Polyphemus has killed Acis, the whole story being a small incident in a blissful world of beauty and peace. The same sense of an interruption of a timeless world by a narrative is present in Beethoven's symphony. Each movement had become successively more engaged in narrative: first the brook and the birds, then the peasants and, finally, the storm. The last movement has no story to tell, the *Hirtengesang* awakening the same sentiments as had been present in the first movement. Remembering once more Beethoven's cautionary 'Mehr Ausdruck der Empfindung als Malerei' the composer is here re-establishing the power of the former over the latter. There has been plenty of painting during the course of the symphony, in turn charming, witty and frightening, but never gratuitous. Now it is time to return to the higher musical quality of feeling.

V Hirtengesang. Frohe, dankbare Gefühle nach dem Sturm
Shepherds' Song. Joyful, grateful feelings after the storm
Allegretto (♩. = 60), F major, 𝄴

Although the fifth movement regains the mood of the first, that mood is not exactly the same; after all, it is now 'nach dem Sturm'. Accordingly, while the movement shares many of the features of the first movement – simple harmonic language, slow harmonic rhythm, easy repetition of melodic material and leisurely crescendo passages – there are differences. The crisp rhythms of $\frac{2}{4}$ are replaced with the lilting gait of 𝄴. Secondly, as the title *Hirtengesang* promises, the last movement is vastly more lyrical. The main theme could not be simpler: two four-bar phrases ending with an unambiguous perfect cadence, and an iambic cross-rhythm to end such as might have been produced in a folksong by the word 'Hirte' (shepherd), 'Herde' (flock) or 'Freude' (joy).

While it has never been claimed that the main theme is an actual folksong, a folk origin has been claimed for the material that leads into it (bb. 1–8). It bears a strong resemblance to the *ranz des vaches*, an alpine horn call to summon the cattle in the region of Rigi in Switzerland.[20] But given the wide distribution of such themes and the propensity of art music to invent themes in this mode when appropriate – the one in Haydn's *Seasons* quoted in Ex. 1 would undoubtedly have been known to Beethoven – it is likely that the resemblance is generic rather than particular.[21]

Having established the essential character of the movement Beethoven clearly needs to enhance it, that is to make the mood even more relaxed. Accordingly, rather than another movement in sonata form, the third, the composer opts for a rondo form so that the music can return with increasing security and comfort to the main theme. The structure of this movement is one usually termed sonata-rondo, but the nineteenth-century formulation of this term is so beset with problems that it is more appropriate to begin with the simple base of a sectional rondo, drawing attention to those features that derive from the more organic structure of sonata form (see Table 4).

The structure of each A section is repetitive, yielding a greater sense of stasis than was apparent in either of the first two movements. In A1, the theme is heard three times, the second statement beginning *piano* and making a gradual fulfilling crescendo towards the third *fortissimo* statement. There are far more *fortissimo* sections in this movement than in the first and they pose a particular problem for conductors, who have to elicit a richness of sound that is neither intense nor stolid. On the first return of the main section (A2), the number

Table 4

Bars	9–32	32–41	42–64	64–80	80–117
Keys	I	I → V/V	V	I	IV→V/I
Section	A1	Trans.	B1	A2	C

Bars	117–40	140–47	148–64	164–264
Keys	I	I → V/I	I	I
Section	A3	Trans.	B2	Coda

of statements of the theme is reduced to two and the accompaniment is decorated. On the second return (A3) there are again three statements but there is no obvious melody, just filigree decoration, the harmonic structure, the obvious phrase patterns, together with the three dynamic stages of *piano*, *piano* with crescendo, and *fortissimo*, being enough to remind listeners of the theme.

Following the three statements of the theme in A1, the music becomes more organic as it appropriates procedures from sonata form. Using the iambic figure from the end of the main theme the transition elaborates its own thematic course in a faster harmonic rhythm (two chords per bar) and, later, with *sforzando* surface rhythms. Section B (the equivalent of a second subject in a sonata form) arises naturally out of this material; it is characterized by repeated perfect cadences in C major and imitation that spreads downwards through the string section. A repeated two-bar cadence theme is even more aggressive, featuring *piano* and crescendo to a *forte* within a couple of bars (bb. 51–2). The nature of the movement is changing rapidly, becoming increasingly more symphonic than anything found in the first movement. Yet the proportions of the movement are unlike those of a sonata form; the whole of the transition and second subject (B) has taken only thirty-three bars, exactly the duration of the first subject, whereas in an exposition of a sonata form the transition and second subject (i.e. the music that is not in the tonic) will normally be much longer than the first subject. By restricting the scope of these paragraphs Beethoven is able to contain the destructive nature of the material itself, and to return the music with conviction to F major and the main theme. To enhance the lure of the main theme, Beethoven includes also the preparatory bars, sustained dominant harmony with the melodic figures now shared between flute, oboe, clarinet and horn.

The second statement of the main theme in A2 is redirected onto the dominant of B♭ in readiness for the second episode, C. It is at this point that the textbook definition of a sonata-rondo becomes inappropriate for, instead of developing material, section C is, for the most part, a new and contrasting paragraph; any references it makes to the main theme are in the nature of preparation for its return rather than full-scale development. Clarinets and bassoons proclaim the sense of a new section with a new theme over a new accompaniment (*legato* arpeggios in violas), in shorter phrase lengths (two-bar phrases) and with a new harmonic rhythm (one chord per bar). Its climactic phrases (b. 86 onwards) lead easily to references to the first bar of the main theme while, in a rare outburst of chromatic harmony, the music moves from B♭ to E♭, to D♭, to B♭ minor and thence to the dominant of F. Consequently the dominant preparation for the return of section A is the longest in the movement, eighteen bars of emphasized C major before the music falls onto F major and the main theme. The orchestration is carefully weighted so that there is a gradual thinning of texture from the rich *fortissimo* in b. 107 to the translucent delicacy of the theme in b. 117, the continuing semiquavers providing a seamless continuity.

The coda forms over a third of the movement. It has two apparently conflicting aims: to provide a sense of apotheosis, and to provide a sense of calm that is appropriate to the *Frohe und dankbare Gefühle* and to the feeling of *Erinnerung* that is the ultimate goal of the symphony. Working out these objectives explains why the coda is so long. The sense of moving towards a summary rather than a mere consolidation is reflected in the complete absence of a full statement of the main theme. Up to this point there have been eight full statements (the most of any single theme in the entire symphony); the coda deals only with the ingredients of the main theme together with the *ranz des vaches*.

In the same way that A2 had unwound the tension generated by the end of the transition and second subject (B1) areas, the coda has to unwind the tension of the immediately preceding transition and the recapitulation (B2). To achieve this Beethoven takes up an even more distant harmonic perspective on the home key of F major; the preparatory bars move to the dominant of the dominant (G major) before falling after five-and-a-half bars to the dominant of F. Bassoons and cellos alone begin the main theme in a confident manner, only to retreat in the second half of the phrase into a *piano* dynamic. Imitative entries deflect the music onto the secondary dominant chord of the supertonic (V/ii), a fresh view of the main theme. A crescendo leads to a *fortissimo* tutti, underpinned by arpeggios derived from the motif that the cellos and bassoons had so cleverly drawn attention to when they withdrew into a *piano* dynamic a few bars earlier. Now cellos and basses stride confidently across two octaves. But Beethoven once again denies the listener a fulfilling *fortissimo*; he withdraws and goes through the same process again, differently scored and with some crucial adjustments in timing: ten bars of preparation, first on V/V and then on V/I; cellos and bassoons play a decorated version of their unison passage (a reference back to the the third statement in A3, b. 133); woodwind instruments make the melodic references to the main theme more explicit; finally, the music arrives once more at the *fortissimo* passage. This is now extended to nineteen glorious bars. There is an increased sense of majestic power: the wide-ranging bass line is now a series of two-bar phrases; the violins reach a melodic peak of G, a tone higher than in the previous paragraph; and the descent from this G incorporates a number of lengthy appoggiaturas. A gradual diminuendo leads into an eight-bar passage that is as serene as the previous passage was glorious. The melodic material is clearly derived from the main theme, but there is now no momentum in the accompaniment, not even a single pizzicato, just sustained *sotto voce* chords. The cadence is repeated with increasing emphasis on a held dominant chord. Beethoven shows for the last time his mastery of harmonic rhythm as the dominant chord is extended to a full five bars (bb. 253–7), followed by seven bars of tonic. Examination of the autograph shows that two of the tonic bars were added at the last moment (bb. 258–9); at first the music went from the dominant chord of b. 257 into the tonic and the horn solo in b. 260. The sound of the muted horn provides that final sense of a receding perspective.

Between 1812 and 1818 Beethoven kept a notebook in which he recorded aphorisms and lengthier passages of prose that had caught his attention, together with some trivia and thoughts of his own. In the last category belongs the remark 'Ruhe und Freyheit sind die größten Guter' ('Tranquillity and freedom are the greatest treasures').[22] Many works that are contemporary with the *Pastoral Symphony*, such as the Fifth Symphony and the first version of the opera *Fidelio*, deal directly with freedom as an attainable consequence of heroic struggle. There is nothing actively heroic about the *Pastoral Symphony*; neither is it passively escapist. In it Beethoven achieves both tranquillity and freedom.

6

Mehr Malerei als Empfindung
Some critical views

The history of the *Pastoral Symphony* in the nineteenth and twentieth
centuries is one in which Beethoven's concerns about its reception in 1808
were realized. The work became as popular as any of the composer's nine
symphonies. Occasionally its content was trivialized, sometimes the work was
patronized, but even when it was admired a greater emphasis was placed on
the programmatic content than Beethoven desired.

One of the earliest extended appreciations of the work appeared in the
Zeitung für die elegante Welt, a journal published in Leipzig. The issue for
Thursday 5 July 1810 contains an essay by one Friedrich Mosengeil of
Meiningen in which Beethoven is identified as the poet, the central figure in
his own five-act drama.[1]

Second Act. Scene by the brook

The poet pauses by the brook – comfortably supported by his lyre – gazing excitedly
at the flowers caught by the breeze , and the clean, blue depths of the sky. The gentle
waves of the brook murmur and splash, and the shadows of the alder trees spread
through the entire scene.

He who cannot or does not want to follow the flight of imagination of the master finds
in this incomparable movement too much uniformity perhaps; he will no doubt fall
asleep from boredom if he does not have an ear for the peaceful brook and the unending
murmurs, and no eye for the unendingly ceaseless ripples.

Our poet awakes! – In the seamless simmering and surging, in which strings and wind
instruments partake, an enchanting kingdom of sounds is perceived. As in the previous
act we hear now and again in this act the fleeting voice of a passing songstress; prevailing
here are the sweet throats of birds. They twitter and coo in the branches, on the ground
the quail enchants, while from on high the trilling of the ascending lark is heard. Finally
the nightingale, quail and cuckoo unite in a trio, which, though disappointingly brief,
is so captivating that he forgives the master for ending soon afterwards. 'Nothing more
beautiful' he believes 'is possible'.

From featuring the poet as the central figure in the work it was a short step
to placing Beethoven, the country-lover, at the centre of the work. In 1833

Johann Peter Lyser (1803–70) provided a drawing for a pocketbook aimed at the musical amateur, *Cäcilia*. It shows Beethoven, with pencil and notebook in hand (not the lyre of Mosengeil's description), reclining on the banks of a stream, composing the *Pastoral Symphony*. Lyser lived in Hamburg and had never met Beethoven, but this picture stimulated a host of imitations, providing an image of the composer which, while not a complete distortion (he did after all sketch on walks in the country), placed him at the centre of the symphony in a way that he would have found alien.[2]

Robert Schumann was one person who wanted to separate the revered figure of Beethoven from the images created by his music. His reverence for the composer led him to propose that a monument be built in the form of a temple, each of the symphonies being represented by a Greek God, Clio for the *Eroica* and Euterpe for the *Pastoral*, with Beethoven as the God Apollo.[3] Of the *Pastoral Symphony* he wrote,

In composing his *Pastoral Symphony* Beethoven well understood the dangers he incurred. His explanatory remark, 'Rather expressive of the feeling than tone painting', contains an entire aesthetic system for composers. And it is absurd for painters to portray him sitting beside a brook, his head in his hands, listening to the babbling water. When Beethoven conceived and carried out his idea for the *Pastoral Symphony*, it was not a single short spring day that inspired him to utter his cry of joy, but the dark commingling of lofty songs above us (as Heine, I believe somewhere says). The manifold voices of creation stirred within him.[4]

These remarks were written in 1835. Within a few years Schumann had written his First Symphony, the 'Spring', a work inspired by a poem by Adolf Böttger but palpably influenced by Beethoven's *Pastoral Symphony* too. At first the four movements of the symphony were headed, *Frühlingsbeginn* (*Coming of Spring*), *Abend* (*Evening*), *Frohe Gespielen* (*Merry Playmates*) and *Voller Frühling* (*Fullness of Spring*), but he later withdrew these headings. In a letter to Spohr, Schumann explained his desire to avoid images that might encourage too graphic a view of the work, sentiments which Beethoven would have appreciated.[5]

I composed this symphony at the end of the winter, with that springtime *élan* that returns every year, right into old age. I did not attempt to depict or describe anything, but the season in which it was born did, I am sure, affect the shape it took and help to make it what it is.

Berlioz's *Symphonie Fantastique* is another work that shows the influence of Beethoven's *Pastoral Symphony*. He is known to have studied the work in some detail in 1829,[6] and its five-movement structure together with the idea of a scenic content may well have played a part in the formation of the *Symphonie Fantastique*. The only ostensibly pastoral movement is the *Scène aux champs*, an adagio in $\frac{6}{8}$ time that opens with a *ranz des vaches* played by two shepherds. Later in the movement Berlioz reproduces the motifs associated with Beethoven's nightingale and quail (b. 67 onwards). Unlike Beethoven, Berlioz was anxious to place the individual at the centre of his work: it is entitled *Episode in the life of an artist* and there is a detailed programme that matches the music throughout. When, later in his life, Berlioz wrote appreciative essays on all nine of Beethoven's symphonies the combination of general hero-worshipping and a willingness to indulge his responses to the music produced an extraordinarily imaginative and passionate account of the *Pastoral Symphony*. But in all this extravagance it is noticeable that Berlioz never makes the symphony an episode in the life of Beethoven, though he does indulge the image that the composer created the slow movement 'whilst reclining on the grass'.

This astonishing landscape seems as if it were the joint work of Poussin and Michael Angelo. A desire to depict the calm of the country-side and the shepherd's gentle ways now actuates the composer of 'Fidelio' and of the 'Eroica' . . .

The herdsmen begin to appear in the fields. They have their usual careless manner, and the sound of their pipes proceeds from far and near. Delightful phrases greet you, like the perfumed morning breeze; and swarms of chattering birds in flight pass rustling overhead. From time to time the atmosphere seems charged with vapour; great clouds appear and hide the sun; then, all at once, they disappear; and there suddenly falls upon both tree and wood the torrent of dazzling light . . .

I despair of being able to give an idea of this prodigious movement [the Storm]. It must be heard in order to form an idea of the degree of truth and sublimity descriptive music can attain in the hands of a man like Beethoven. Listen! – listen to those rain-charged squalls of wind; to the dull grumblings of the basses, also to the keen whistling of the piccolo, which announces to us that a horrible tempest is on the point of breaking out. The hurricane approaches and grows in force; an immense chromatic feature, starting from the heights of the instrumentation, pursues its course until it gropes its way to the lowest orchestral depths. There it secures the basses, dragging them with it upwards; the whole shuddering like a whirlwind sweeping everything before it. Then, the trombones burst forth, the thunder of the kettledrums becomes redoubled in violence, it is no longer merely rain and wind, but an awful cataclysm, the universal deluge – the end of the world.

This literally produces giddiness; and many people, when they hear this storm, can scarcely tell whether their emotion is one of pleasure of or pain . . .

How the antique poems, however beautiful or admired they may be, pale in significance when compared with this marvel of modern music. Theocritus and Virgil were great in singing the praises of landscape beauty . . .

But this poem of Beethoven! – these long periods so richly coloured! – these living pictures! – these perfumes! – that light! – that eloquent silence! – that vast horizon! – those enchanted nooks secreted in the woods! – that harvest of gold! – those golden harvests! – those rose-tinted clouds like wandering flecks upon the surface of the sky! – that immense plain seeming to slumber beneath the rays of the mid-day sun! – Man is absent, and Nature alone reveals itself to admiration.[7]

Liszt published piano reductions of all Beethoven's symphonies; that for the *Pastoral Symphony* was prepared in 1837 when he and Marie d'Agoult were guests at George Sand's country house in Nohant. His recitals often included a performance of the last three movements as a kind of symphonic poem for piano, the Storm, in particular, exploring to the full the sonority of the mid-nineteenth-century piano. Generally, Liszt's reduction is very faithful to Beethoven's original, though he does permit himself a few *fff* markings in the Storm and the finale, where Beethoven was content with *ff*, plus the occasional *martellato* and *marcatissimo*. In a letter written in 1841 to Marie d'Agoult he expressed his admiration for the work: 'Put the Golden Fleece on one side of a table and the *Pastoral Symphony* on the other, and allow me the choice between carrying off the former or writing the latter – and I shall not hesitate for a single moment'.[8]

As many writers have noted, Liszt's own attitude to programme music derived from the one espoused by Beethoven in the *Pastoral Symphony*, an emphasis on mood and atmosphere, rather than on narrative detail informing most of the composer's symphonic poems. The only work to share Beethoven's subject matter was, significantly, the first, *Ce qu'on entend sur la montagne*, though there are no direct echoes of the *Pastoral Symphony*.

One of the most bizarre aspects of the performance history of Beethoven's symphony are the many recorded instances in the nineteenth century of performances with scenery and action. A concert given at the King's Theatre in London in June 1829, only a couple of years after the death of the composer, contained Handel's *Acis and Galatea* in the first half, and a visual presentation by actors and dancers of the *Pastoral Symphony* in the second half.[9] When in 1832, in Lyons, Berlioz saw a similar performance his response was that 'It was like seeing in a brothel the portrait of some adored angel of one's dreams'.[10] In 1863 the newly rejuvenated *Allgemeine musikalische Zeitung* reported disdainfully on a recent stage performance of the *Pastoral Symphony* in Düsseldorf, making the fundamental point that a picture is a picture and a symphony is a symphony, and that this kind of presentation did not allow either art form to exert its potential. The critique included a synopsis of the action.[11]

As in the symphony, the representation falls into three main parts. The first picture shows a serene countryside in summer bathed in the light of morning, on the left a distant perspective, on the right a copse with a grazing flock and attendant shepherds. Harvesters approach and begin their work, the parish priest appears, a visiting family from the town strolls around and moves towards the village. Midday and the departure of the harvesters mark the end of the first sequence. The second movement begins, and the countryside changes its appearance to give the spectator a new outlook: a charming valley between wooded hills through which a brook flows; overhanging trees with the summer sun streaming through the leaves. Wood-gathering children appear and play by the brook; the townspeople enter, the parents rest themselves in the shade, two young lovers gather flowers and catch butterflies, resting finally on the grass. With this harmonious, peaceful, idyllic group the second movement ends. For the third movement we find ourselves in the middle of the village in front of the inn, where the peasants are dancing merrily; a squabble interrupts the dance; it's resolved and the dance begins anew; but the storm threatens. Everybody disappears and only appropriate scenic effects accompany the music. The storm passes over, a rainbow appears, one-by-one the peasants step out of their houses, the sun sets slowly casting its final rays on the church roof; the priest enters and, as the evening bell tolls, the people offer their prayers. With this scene the performance comes to an end.

Wagner held ambivalent views about the *Pastoral Symphony*. He knew the work intimately, both from private piano performances (solo and duet) and from conducting the work. One remark about the tempo of the slow movement suggests that many contemporary performances were very sluggish: 'They don't know the difference between andante and adagio, they drag movements that ought to flow and ruin them that way'.[12]

Following a performance by Anton Rubinstein on the piano Cosima Wagner faithfully recorded her husband's remarks. 'One must take care not to fall into emotional accents with it . . . He deplores the repeats, which make it all sound insignificant, and finds the whole thing has something of the spirit of 18th-century *bergerie*. At one point he quotes Polonius: "Pastoral, pastoral-comical, tragical-comical-pastoral".'[13]

On another occasion, in a conversation with the author Heinrich von Stein that ranged over the spiritual qualities of art from different epochs, Wagner expressed his admiration for Beethoven's work as a potential force for good.

'I am coming closer to your view: human beings do not have to be so evil, I know what needs to be done in order to regenerate them, and then we shall play them the *Pastoral Symphony*!' – 'They will have long to wait, as Schleinitz says, before they get an emperor like that.' – 'Before they get a God as good as that,' I [Cosima Wagner] say.[14]

Wagner's firm views about the performance of Beethoven's symphonies, in matters of detail as well as in conception, produced a celebrated essay on the

Ninth Symphony. This was the starting point for Felix Weingartner's essays on all nine of the symphonies and, taking his cue from Wagner, they are largely concerned with adjusting the orchestration to take advantage of chromatic horns and trumpets, and, blithely stated, to correct the misjudgements that the composer had made because of deficient hearing. For the *Pastoral Symphony* doubling the wind parts in the last two movements is suggested, horns are added to bb. 217–27 of the first movement and various passages for the instruments in the Storm are rewritten; many of the other adjustments to the phrasing, accentuation and articulation seem to be the inevitable result of Weingartner's own recommendations, trying to get the music to speak through the bloated sound of his own enlarged orchestra. On the other hand Weingartner condemned other amendments that seem to have gained some currency.

This wonderful transition [from the Storm to the finale] will bear a gradual slackening of the time until the entry of the pastoral song, for which ♩. = 60 is a very good metronome mark. I cannot warn strongly enough against playing the last notes of the flute solo an octave higher and thus bringing it up to the high C. It is precisely the interval of the seventh between the high A and the lower B that generates so much warmth and charm . . .

Legend tells of a conductor who added kettledrums in this [last] movement. If this be true, no word can express the barbarism of such a proceeding. Surely no supreme genius, only common sense, is needed to perceive that in this symphony Beethoven has reserved the kettledrums exclusively to produce the noise of thunder and with inimitable fine-feeling has abstained from using them on any other occasion.[15]

Debussy attended a performance of the *Pastoral Symphony* conducted by Weingartner at the Concert Lamoureux in Paris in 1903. He was dismissive of the conductor's fastidious approach but, more surprisingly, he was even more dismissive, to the point of rudeness, of the work itself, allowing himself to become obsessed with the particularities of the programme and claiming a complete dislocation between Beethoven's perception of nature and nature itself.

Last Sunday was an irresistibly pleasant day. The first sunlight of the year seemed to forestall any attempt to listen to music, no matter what it was. A day for the swallows to return . . .

M. Weingartner chose this day to conduct the orchestra at the Concert Lamoureux. Well, we can't all be perfect!

All the famours ears of Paris were there on the alert: eccentric rich old ladies, corseted young dilettantes, and wizened old men – the very best of audiences, ripe for anyone who knew how to use it. Weingartner has for a long time known how to be certain of an enthusiastic reception. First of all, he conducted the *Pastoral* Symphony with the care of a meticulous gardener. Every weed, every caterpillar was painstakingly removed! It was all done with such refinement that it seemed like one of those glossy, finely detailed paintings where the gentle undulation of the hills is made of twopenny velvet and the trees are formed with curling irons.

All in all, the popularity of the *Pastoral* Symphony rests upon the common and mutual misunderstanding that exists between man and nature. Look at that scene by the brook! . . . A brook where, apparently, the oxen come to drink. At least, that's what the sound of the bassoons suggests to me. Not to mention the wooden nightingale and the Swiss cuckoo-clock cuckoo – more like the art of M. de Vaucauson than drawn from nature's book. All such imitations are in the end useless – purely arbitrary interpretations.

But certain of the old master's pages do contain expression more profound than the beauty of the landscape. Why? Simply because there is no attempt at direct imitation, but rather at capturing the *invisible* sentiments of nature. Does one render the mystery of the forest by recording the height of the trees? It is more a process where the limitless depths of the forest give free rein to the imagination.

Elsewhere in this symphony, Beethoven shows himself to be of a time when one never saw the world of nature except in books. This is proved by the "storm", which forms part of this same piece. The real terror of man and beast in the face of a storm is hidden beneath the folds of a romantic cloak, and the thunder is hardly severe.

But it would be stupid to think that I have no respect for Beethoven. It's just that a musician of genius, such as he, can make unconscious mistakes greater than anyone else. There is no man who is bound to write only masterpieces, and if we class the *Pastoral Symphony* as one of these, then we have no yardstick with which to measure the others. That's all I want to say.[16]

Many people, including the author, were introduced to the *Pastoral Symphony* as part of the film *Fantasia*, which first appeared in 1940. It constitutes one of the longest sequences in the film, music from all five movements (heavily cut in certain cases) accompanying the cartoon cavortings of friendly fawns, doe-eyed nymphs, jolly Bacchus and nasty Thor. In a sense it represents an up-dating of the nineteenth-century staged performances, even down to such details as the appearance of a rainbow at the end of the storm. Together, Stokowski and Hollywood managed to reduce the work to the level of kitsch.

This brief survey has concentrated, perhaps misleadingly, on posterity's unsympathetic, sometimes distorted view of the symphony. Many performances in the nineteenth and twentieth centuries were no doubt presented and received in a more neutral fashion guided, at least, by the overriding and serious-minded sentiment that this was a symphony by one of the acknowledged geniuses of music. Of the many pages of prose written in the English language about the work those by George Grove and Donald Tovey are notable for pointing the reader towards an appropriate and sympathetic response to the work, with what might be summarized as scholarly inquisitiveness in the case of the former and natural empathy in the latter.

George Grove's book *Beethoven and his Nine Symphonies* appeared in 1896. His chapter on the *Pastoral Symphony* deals sympathetically with Beethoven's love of nature, mentions the importance of Haydn's *Creation*, shows an interest in the information that the various authentic musical sources shed on the work and presents a readable account of the progress of the work.[17] Tovey's essay is one of his finest, over twelve pages outlining the structure and content of the music. He is particularly concerned with the issue that preoccupied Beethoven and often misled posterity: the part played by musical painting.[18]

In the whole symphony there is not a note of which the musical value would be altered if cuckoos and nightingales, and country folk, and thunder and lightning, and the howling and whistling of the wind, were things that had never been named by man, either in connexion with music or with anything else. Whether we have words for common objects and events of the countryside or whether we have no words, there are feelings evoked by these objects in proportion to our intelligent susceptibility; and the great master of any language, whether that language be music, painting, sculpture, architecture, or speech, can invoke the deepest part of these feelings in his own terms. And his art will always remain pure as long as he holds to Beethoven's dictum; which may be philosophically re-translated 'more the expression of feelings than the illustration of things'.

Sixty years have elapsed since Tovey's essay first appeared in print, and most modern listeners are more than willing to share the author's outlook on the work, discarding the trivial and distorted images of previous generations. Beethoven's popularity, too, is changing. He is no longer viewed solely as a heroic figure who transformed music but as a composer who interacted strongly with his cultural and musical background, as much the product of the late eighteenth century as he was the creator of the nineteenth. Judged by Beethoven's own criteria for the *Pastoral Symphony*, the immediate and posthumous reception accorded to it suggests a failure. While the inspiration for the work drew on a long heritage of the pastoral in music its reception almost immediately ensnared it in Romanticism. It will never be possible to recapture the atmosphere in the Theater an der Wien on 22 December 1808. But if we allow that from his own experience Beethoven was producing a work that was charming, naive, simple and, above all, wonderfully secure, then the work might begin to exercise an appeal that is closer to the composer's aspirations.

Notes

1 The concert of 22 December 1808

1 For a full account of the concert see E. Forbes (rev. and ed.), *Thayer's Life of Beethoven* (Princeton, New Jersey, 1967), pp. 446–9; and H. C. Robbins Landon, *Beethoven: A Documentary Study* (London, 1970), pp. 223–4.

2 No copy of the original handbill has survived. Its content was reproduced in a short report of the concert in the *Allgemeine musikalische Zeitung*, 11 (1808–9), cols. 267–8. The sub-heading of the *Pastoral Symphony*, *Reminiscence of country life* (*Erinnerung an das Landleben*), and the title *Shepherds' Song* (*Hirtengesang*) for the last movement are present in the autograph and in the parts used for the first performance but they are not included in the transcription. In the absence of the original handbill it is impossible to determine whether the transcription is fully accurate. The headings for the first and last movements of the *Pastoral Symphony* differ slightly from those finally chosen. See chapter 3, pp. 37–43.

2 Background

1 M. S. Morrow, *Concert Life in Haydn's Vienna: Aspects of a Developing Musical and Social Institution* (Stuyvesant, New York, 1989), pp. 93–8, pp. 305–40.

2 O. Biba, 'Beethoven und die "Liebhaber Concerte" in Wien im Winter 1807/08' in *Beiträge '76–78: Beethoven-Kolloquium 1977: Dokumentation und Aufführungspraxis*, ed. R. Klein (Kassel, 1978), pp. 82–93.

3 *Allgemeine musikalische Zeitung*, 9 (1806–7), col. 400.

4 M.S. Morrow, *Concert Life*, p. 295, p. 297.

5 Ibid., pp. 344–59.

6 Ibid., pp. 401–3.

7 See the following three essays: J. Macek, 'Franz Joseph Maximilian Lobkowitz. Musikfreund und Kunstmäzen'; T. Volek and J. Macek, 'Beethoven und Lobkowitz'; and J. Fojtíková and T. Volek, 'Die Beethoveniana der Lobkowitz-Musiksammlung und ihre Kopisten'. All are contained in S. Brandenburg and M. Gutiérrez-Denhoff (eds.), *Beethoven und Böhmen. Beiträge zu Biographie und Wirkungsgeschichte Beethovens* (Bonn, 1988), respectively pp. 147–201, pp. 203–17 and pp. 219–58. See also T. Volek and J. Macek, 'Beethoven's Rehearsals at the Lobkowitz's', *Musical Times*, 127 (1986), pp. 75–80.

8 My translation of the original quoted in M. S. Morrow, *Concert Life*, p. 507.

9 The table is based on the calendar of performances given in M. S. Morrow, *Concert Life*, pp. 303–64. Sometimes the sources do not clearly state how many symphonies were performed. Overtures by Mozart and Beethoven are omitted; it is possible that some of the works by the lesser composers were actually overtures or works not scored for an orchestra.

10 The foregoing is indebted to the full account of Eberl's career and his symphonies given in *The Symphony 1720–1840*, editor-in-chief B. S. Brook, series B vol. IX (New York and

London, 1983), pp. xxx–xlii, pp. xlvii–xlix. A score of the E♭ symphony is to be found on pp. 243–317.

11 For a convenient list of these performances see A. Peter Brown, *Performing Haydn's The Creation* (Bloomington, Indiana, 1986), pp. 2–7.

12 See M. S. Morrow, *Concert Life*, p. 311–52.

13 A. Sandberger, 'Zu den Geschichtlichen Voraussetzungen der Beethoven'schen Pastoral Sinfonie', *Bulletin de la Société 'Union Musicologique'*, 3 (1923), pp. 133–85.

14 M. Germer, *The Austro-Bohemian Pastorella and Pastoral Mass to c1780* (PhD diss., New York University, 1989).

15 Ibid. Also G. Chew, *The Christmas Pastorella in Austria, Bohemia and Moravia* (PhD diss., University of Manchester, 1968).

16 G. Nottebohm, *Zweite Beethoveniana* (Leipzig, 1887), p. 378.

17 This work is discussed in G. Chew, *The Christmas Pastorella*, vol. I, pp. 145–51; a score is given in vol. II. The work is in a sturdy and highly rhythmic C major, rather reminiscent of the first movement of the C major piano concerto, qualities that may have prompted the attribution to Beethoven.

18 G. Chew, 'The Austrian Pastorella and the *Stylus rusticanus*: Comic and Pastoral Elements in Austrian Music, 1750–1800' in D. W. Jones (ed.), *Music in Eighteenth-Century Austria* (forthcoming, Cambridge, 1996).

19 See *The Symphony 1720–1840*, editor-in-chief B. S. Brook, Reference Volume (New York and London, 1986). A score of Hofmann's *Symphonia Pastorella* in D major is contained in *The Symphony 1720–1840*, series B vol. VII (New York and London, 1984), pp. 105–19.

20 James Webster has provided a convenient summary of this repertoire plus a penetrating account of the implications it has for modern understanding of the period in *Haydn's 'Farewell' Symphony and the Idea of Classical Style. Through-Composition and Cyclic Integration in His Instrumental Music* (Cambridge, 1991), pp. 225–49.

21 Score in *The Symphony 1720–1840*, series B vol. X (New York and London, 1981), pp. 399–425.

22 *La Primavera. Sinfonia in F . . . Composta dal Signore F. A. Hoffmeister* (Vienna, 1793), RISM A1/4, H5894; date of publication from A. Weinmann, *Die Wiener Verlagswerke von Franz Anton Hoffmeister* (Beiträge zur Geschichte des alt-Wiener Musikverlages, 2/8) (Vienna, 1964), p. 154.

23 Published in *Selected Orchestral Works of Karl Ditters von Dittersdorf*, ed. J Liebeskind (reprint: New York, 1971), pp. 59–82.

24 Score: Diletto Musicale No. 259, ed. W. Jerger (Vienna and Munich, 1972).

25 *The Symphony 1720–1840*, Reference Volume, p. 547.

26 Ibid., p. 547.

27 F-J. Fétis, 'Knecht', in *Biographie Universelle des Musiciens et Bibliographie Générale de la Musique* (Paris, 1837–44), vol. V, p. 62. 'Deux Symphonies Pastorales' in *Revue et Gazette Musicale de Paris*, 33 (1866), pp. 337–40.

28 A. Weinmann, *Johann Traeg. Die Anzeigen des Kopiaturbetriebes Johann Traeg in der Wiener Zeitung zwischen 1782 und 1805* (Wiener Archivstudien, VI) (Vienna, 1981), p. 33. Weinmann, *Johann Traeg. Die Musikalienverzeichnisse von 1799 und 1804* (Beiträge zur Geschichte des alt-Wiener Musikverlages, 2/17) (Vienna, 1973), p. 15.

29 See the inventory of Beethoven's estate given in E. Forbes (rev. and ed.) *Thayer's Life of Beethoven*, pp. 1061–76.

30 The original French is given in A. Sandberger, 'Zu den Geschichtlichen Voraussetzungen der Beethoven'schen Pastoralsinfonie', p. 176. Several exemplars of the Bossler publication have survived; see RISM A1/5, K961.

31 E. Anderson (trans. and ed.), *The Letters of Beethoven* (London, 1961), vol. I, p. 60.

32 Ibid., vol. I, p. 161.

33 Ibid., vol. I, p. 234.

34 Ibid., vol. I, p. 273.
35 Ibid., vol. I, p. 420.
36 Ibid., vol. I, p. 423.
37 Ibid., vol. II, p. 500.
38 E. Forbes (rev. and ed.), *Thayer's Life of Beethoven*, pp. 702–3.
39 A. F. Schindler, *Beethoven as I Knew Him* (translation by C. S. Jolly of *Biographie von Ludwig Beethoven*, edited by D. W. MacArdle) (London, 1966), pp. 34–5, p. 134, p. 143, p. 248, p. 365. The passages of Sturm copied out by Beethoven are given in L. Nohl, *Beethovens Brevier*, 2nd, ed. P. Sakolowski (Leipzig, 1901), pp. 111–46.
40 Translation from *Reflections on the Works of God and of his Providence throughout all Nature. From the German of Mr C. C. Sturm*. Revised by Dr Collyer (London, 1824), vol. II, pp. 13–15.
41 Translation: ibid., pp. 402-4.
42 The relationship between this song and the *Pastoral Symphony* is discussed in B. Cooper, *Beethoven and the Creative Process* (Oxford, 1990), p. 56, p. 63.

3 Genesis and reception

1 G. Nottebohm, *Zweite Beethoveniana*, p. 375.
2 R. W. Wade, 'Beethoven's Eroica Sketchbook', *Fontes Artis Musicae*, 23 (1976), pp. 254–89.
3 B. Cooper, *Beethoven and the Creative Process*, p. 80.
4 'Einfach, ruhig, heiter und gemütlich, beinahe im *pastoralen* Style . . .' C. Czerny, *Über den richtigen Vortrag der sämtlichen Beethoven'schen Klavierwerke*, ed. P. Badura-Skoda (Vienna, 1963), p. 111. Czerny's comment on the slow movement ('One cannot help thinking of an antique tragic scene') is part of a welter of circumstantial evidence Owen Jander uses to suggest that the slow movement is a depiction of Orpheus taming the Furies (as first suggested by Adolf Bernhard Marx in 1859), and, moreover, that the whole concerto deals with the Orpheus legend. As Jander frankly admits, this thesis is unprovable, yet his exploration of possible extra-musical stimuli in this work is a valuable counterbalance to the puritanical view of Beethoven as a composer of highly abstract instrumental music. O. Jander, 'Beethoven's "Orpheus in Hades": The *Andante con moto* of the Fourth Concerto', *19th Century Music*, 8 (1984–85), pp. 195–212.
5 E. Anderson (trans. and ed.), *The Letters of Beethoven*, vol. I, p. 192.
6 DSB Landsberg 12. See D. Johnson, A. Tyson and R. Winter, *The Beethoven Sketchbooks* (Oxford, 1985), p. 157.
7 All the sketches except that for the last mentioned are reproduced in G. Nottebohm, *Zweite Beethoveniana*, pp. 370–1. He seems to have regarded the last mentioned as ideas for the accompaniment of the slow movement; hence his implication that sketches for all five movements are contained in this source.
8 Like other sketchbooks by the composer it was dismembered in the nineteenth century. The main portion is now held by the British Library (henceforward referred to as Pastoral Symphony London) and a substantial number of leaves is held by the Staatsbibliothek zu Berlin – Preußische Kulturbesitz (henceforward Pastoral Symphony Landsberg 10); single leaves are found in other libraries. For full details see A. Tyson, 'A Reconstruction of the Pastoral Symphony Sketchbook (British Museum Add. MS 31766)' in *Beethoven Studies I* (London, 1974), pp. 67–96; and D. Johnson, A. Tyson and R. Winter, *The Beethoven Sketchbooks*, pp. 166–73. A modern transcription (with commentary) of the London portion is available: D. Weise (ed.), *Beethoven. Ein Skizzenbuch zur Pastoralsymphonie Op. 68 und zu den Trios Op. 70, 1 und 2* (Bonn, 1961), 2 vols. Nicholas Marston is preparing a new edition of the complete sketchbook. I am grateful to him for allowing me to consult his microfilm collection of the sources and giving information and advice so freely.
9 Some of these annotations are given in G. Nottebohm, *Zweite Beethoveniana*, pp. 375, and in

the preface to the Eulenburg score. A fuller list (including annotations from Pastoral Symphony Landsberg 10) is given in D. Weise, *Beethoven. Ein Skizzenbuch zur Pastoralsymphonie*, vol. II, p. 11, p. 17.

10 F. E. Kirby, 'Beethoven's Pastoral Symphony as a *Sinfonia caracteristica*', *Musical Quarterly*, 56 (1970), pp. 605–23.

11 D. G. Türk, *School of Clavier Playing*, trans. R. H. Haggh (Lincoln and London, 1982), p. 388, p. 385.

12 See *Joseph Haydn in seiner Zeit* (Eisenstadt, 1982), p. 488.

13 E. Forbes (rev. and ed.), *Thayer's Life of Beethoven*, p. 620.

14 This general remark was prompted by the view that the finale of the 'Appassionata' sonata (Op. 57) depicted a stormy sea at night, during which a distant cry for help is heard. C. Czerny, *Über den richtigen Vortrag*, p. 54.

15 A. F. Schindler, *Beethoven as I Knew Him*, p. 407.

16 See p. 65, pp. 70–1 and p. 72.

17 Quoted in N. Zaslaw, *Mozart's Symphonies. Context, Performance Practice, Reception* (Oxford, 1989), p. 237.

18 Translation from H. C. Robbins Landon, *Haydn: Chronicle and Works. Haydn: The Late Years* (London, 1977), p. 189.

19 M. S. Morrow, *Concert Life*, p. 348.

20 Ibid., p. 323, pp. 334–5.

21 Ibid., p. 313.

22 See the extracts quoted in H. C. Robbins Landon, *Haydn: the Late Years*, p. 189; and Landon, *Haydn: Chronicle and Works. Haydn: The Years of 'The Creation' 1796–1800* (London, 1977), p. 594.

23 E. Anderson (trans. and ed.), *The Letters of Beethoven*, vol. I, pp. 188–9.

24 Ibid., vol. I, p. 190.

25 Wilhelm Rust's letter to his sister. See E. Forbes (rev. and ed.), *Thayer's Life of Beethoven*, p. 439, p. 441, p. 474.

26 See E. Anderson (trans. and ed.), *The Letters of Beethoven*, vol. I, pp. 191–2.

27 S. Brandenburg, 'Die Stichvorlage zur Erstausgabe von Beethovens Pastoralsymphonie op. 68: eine neuaufgefundene Primärquelle' in *Festschrift Rudolph Elvers*, eds. E. Herttrich and H. Schneider (Tutzing, 1985), pp. 49–61.

28 The practice is alluded to in Dittersdorf's letter to Artaria (8 September 1788) in which he explores the possibility of the firm publishing six recent symphonies after a period of six months; see J. LaRue, 'Dittersdorf Negotiates a Price' in *Hans Albrecht in memoriam*, eds. W. Brennecke and H. Haase (Kassel, 1962), pp. 156–7. Beethoven's Op. 59 quartets were published a year after the dedicatee, Count Razumovsky, had received them; E. Forbes (rev. and ed.), *Thayer's Life of Beethoven*, p. 408.

29 J. Fojtíková and T. Volek, 'Die Beethoveniana der Lobkowitz-Musiksammlung und ihre Kopisten', p. 232, pp. 245–6.

30 Ibid., pp. 243–5.

31 E. Anderson (trans. and ed.), *The Letters of Beethoven*, vol. I, p. 199. Anderson's tentative inference that the Pastoral Symphony, too, was at some point intended for Oppersdorff has no documentary basis. Also, Forbes's statement that the 'someone else' was Breitkopf and Härtel is disproved by this discovery; see E. Forbes (rev. and ed.), *Thayer's Life of Beethoven*, p. 434.

32 E. Anderson (trans. and ed.), *The Letters of Beethoven*, vol. I, p. 186.

33 D. Weise (ed.), *Ein Skizzenbuch zur Chorfantasie op. 80 und zu anderen Werken* (Bonn, 1957), p. 12, p. 92.

34 *Allgemeine musikalische Zeitung*, 11 (1808–9), col. 267. A transcription of the headings and titles written on the violin part used in the first performance is given in G. Nottebohm, *Zweite Beethoveniana*, p. 378.

35 E. Forbes (rev. and ed.), *Thayer's Life of Beethoven*, pp. 446–9; H. C. Robbins Landon, *Beethoven: A Documentary Biography*, pp. 223–4.

36 See E. Forbes (rev. and ed.), *Thayer's Life of Beethoven*, p. 449.

37 J. Fojtíková and T. Volek, 'Die Beethoveniana der Lobkowitz-Musiksammlung und ihre Kopisten', pp. 248–9. The authors' contention that all the parts are marked with a 'W' (for Wranitsky) is unfounded; all carry the initial 'V', the significance of which is not clear. I am grateful to Otto Biba, Director of the Archive of the Gesellschaft der Musikfreunde for forwarding this information at a time when the archive was closed to the public.

38 E. Forbes (rev. and ed.), *Thayer's Life of Beethoven*, pp. 686–8. A facsimile is included in W. Malloch, 'Carl Czerny's Metronome Marks for Haydn and Mozart Symphonies', *Early Music*, 16 (1988), p. 75.

39 In an undated letter Beeethoven, wrote that 'The *Sammler* gave a much better and truer review of the symphony in F and the other symphonies [sic] than the *Musikzeitung*'; E. Anderson (trans. and ed.), *The Letters of Beethoven*, vol. III, p. 1447. The review of the *Sammler* is given here for the first time. I am grateful to Else Radant Landon for transcribing it from a copy of the journal in the Stadtbibliothek, Vienna. It is the only source that mentions the presence of Archduke Rudolph at the concert. *Der Sammler* (Thursday, 5 January 1809), p. 8.

40 E. Anderson (trans. and ed.), *The Letters of Beethoven*, vol. I, p. 212.

41 *Allgemeine musikalische Zeitung*, 11 (1808–9), col. 267–9. This reluctance to evaluate Beethoven's music after only one performance is a feature of criticism in the journal; see M. S. Morrow, 'Of Unity and Passion: The Aesthetics of Concert Criticism in Early Nineteenth-Century Vienna', *19th Century Music*, 12 (1990), p. 200.

42 E. Anderson (trans. and ed.), *The Letters of Beethoven*, vol. I, p. 217.

43 The review is in *Allgemeine musikalische Zeitung*, 11 (1808–9), col. 435–7; I have used with slight modifications the translation by J. Rutter in *Beethoven: Classic and Romantic*, Open University A341, block II, units 5–8 (Milton Keynes, 1988), p. 119. Haydn's death was announced in the issue of 21 June; 11 (1808–9), col. 608.

4 Design and orchestration

1 D. Weise (ed.), *Beethoven. Ein Skizzenbuch zur Pastoralsymphonie*, vol. I, p. 14r.

2 These descriptions are taken from the convenient conspectus in R. Steblin, *A History of Key Characteristics in the Eighteenth and Early Nineteenth Centuries* (Ann Arbor, 1983), pp. 260–1.

3 M. Germer, *The Austro-Bohemian Pastorella and Pastoral Mass to c1780*, pp. 442–61; and R. Steblin, *A History of Key Characteristics*, pp. 274–5.

4 E. Forbes (rev. and ed.), *Thayer's Life of Beethoven*, p. 618.

5 'Auf eine Weite von einigen Schritten zu entfernen'. 'Sporck' in E. L. Gerber, *Historisch-biographisches Lexikon der Tonkünstler* (1790–2), vol. II, p. 551. See also H. Fitzpatrick, *The Horn and Horn-Playing and the Austro-Bohemian tradition from 1680 to 1830* (London, 1970), p. 178, p. 204, p. 225.

5 Technique and image

1 'It was very surprising to me, when, listening to the radio recently, I discovered – and later found confirmed in the score – that in the first three movements Beethoven uses almost no minor chords, except in a very small number of cases, when it is impossible, with respect to the natural laws of harmony, to omit minor triads. Even then he uses an escape by leaving many sections in unison, unaccompanied, when the melody is understandable without harmony.' L. Stein (ed.), *Style and Idea. Selected Writings of Arnold Schoenberg* (London, 1975), p. 130.

2 P. Gossett, 'Beethoven's Sixth Symphony: Sketches for the First Movement', *Journal of the American Musicological Society*, 27 (1974), p. 253.

3 Ibid., pp. 253–60.

4 The first author to draw attention to this was G. Grove, *Beethoven and His Nine Symphonies* (London, 1896), p. 223.

5 The conductor Norman Del Mar referred to the 'dangerously thick texture' of the opening and warned against aggravating the situation with too slow a tempo. This is a passage that benefits enormously from performance on period instruments, their lighter attack and sound vindicating Beethoven's ear, whereas modern instruments produce an over-rich sound. N. Del Mar, *Conducting Beethoven. Volume I. The Symphonies* (Oxford, 1992), p. 110.

6 D. Weise, *Beethoven. Ein Skizzenbuch zur Pastoralsymphonie*, vol. I, p. 18v, p. 19r.

7 A. F. Schindler, *Beethoven as I Knew Him*, pp. 144–5. None of the commentary on the *Pastoral Symphony* occurs in the first version of Schindler's biography which appeared in 1840, casting further doubt on its veracity; an English translation by I. Moscheles appeared in 1841 (*The Life of Beethoven*).

8 D. F. Tovey, *Essays in Musical Analysis. Volume I: Symphonies* (London, 1935), pp. 46–7, p. 51.

9 O. Jander, 'The Prophetic Conversation in Beethoven's "Scene by the Brook"', *Musical Quarterly*, 77 (1993), pp. 520–1. Jander has many more intriguing observations on the possible symbolism contained in the movement, postulating a programme that deals with Beethoven's discovery of his deafness and eventual resignation to his fate (ibid., pp. 553–5). To place the composer as the central figure in this movement, in the manner of the poet/musician in Schubert's *Die schöne Müllerin*, seems fundamentally alien to the aesthetic background that shaped the *Pastoral Symphony*. That the work came to be viewed in this way in the nineteenth century there is no denying, but whether Beethoven, as the willing heir to the late eighteenth century, composed it in this manner is doubtful. Like Haydn in *The Creation* and *The Seasons* Beethoven is dealing with universal values not individual torment.

10 D. Weise, *Beethoven. Ein Skizzenbuch zur Pastoralsymphonie*, vol. I, p. 9v.

11 Ibid., p. 18v, p. 18r, p. 20r, p. 22r.

12 S. Brandenburg, 'Once Again: On the Question of the Repeat of the Scherzo and Trio in Beethoven's Fifth Symphony' in *Beethoven Essays. Studies in Honor of Elliot Forbes*, eds. L. Lockwood and P. Benjamin (Harvard, 1984), pp. 146–98.

13 A. F. Schindler, *Beethoven as I Knew Him*, pp. 145–6.

14 B. Cooper (ed.), *The Beethoven Compendium. A Guide to Beethoven's Life and Music* (London, 1991), pp. 224–5.

15 The following number in the ballet, *Jagdlied* (*Hunting Song*), provides a slight melodic foretaste of the D major passage near the opening; however, Beethoven carefully avoids any horn fifths in the symphony.

16 A. F. Schindler, *Beethoven as I Knew Him*, pp. 146–7.

17 D. Weise, *Beethoven. Ein Skizzenbuch zur Pastoralsymphonie*, p. 26v.

18. Ibid., p. 30v.

19 G. Grove, *Beethoven and His Nine Symphonies*, p. 219.

20 A. Hyatt King, 'Mountains, Music, and Musicians', *Musical Quarterly*, 31 (1945), p. 403.

21 The following may be added to the many examples given by Hyatt King; the opening of Xavier Lefèvre's *Hymne à l' Agriculture* first performed in June 1796; I am grateful to David Charlton for bringing this to my attention. A wind sextet in E♭ (*Sestetto Pastorale*) by Franz Krommer includes a theme that is directly modelled on Beethoven's first subject; the work has been recorded on CLAV CD50–9004.

22 M. Solomon, 'Beethoven's Tagebuch of 1812–1818' in *Beethoven Studies 3*, ed. A. Tyson (Cambridge, 1982), p. 269.

6 Mehr Malerei als Empfindung

1 F. Mosengeil, 'Beethoven's Pastoral-Symphonie', *Zeitung für die elegante Welt*, 133 (1810), pp. 1050–1.

2 A. Comini, *The Changing Image of Beethoven. A Study in Mythmaking* (New York, 1987), pp. 85–6. The drawing and a derivative are given as Figs. 50 and 51. They are reproduced also in O. Jander, 'The Prophetic Conversation in Beethoven's "Scene by the Brook"', pp. 532–3.

3 A. Comini, *The Changing Image*, p. 153.

4 As quoted in R. Schumann, *On Music and Musicians* (London, 1946), p. 96.

5 R. Taylor, *Robert Schumann. His Life and Work* (London, 1982), p. 208.

6 D. Cairns, *Berlioz 1803–1832. The Making of an Artist* (London, 1989), p. 287.

7 H. Berlioz (trans. E. Evans), *A Critical Study of Beethoven's Nine Symphonies* (London, 1913), pp. 71–8.

8 As quoted in A. Williams, *Portrait of Liszt by Himself and His Contemporaries* (Oxford, 1990), p. 176.

9 G. Grove, *Beethoven and His Nine Symphonies*, p. 226.

10 D. Cairns, *Berlioz*, p. 499.

11 'Beethoven in Malkasten', *Allgemeine musikalische Zeitung*, 1 (1863), pp. 293–9.

12 M. Gregor-Delling and D. Mack (eds.), G. Skelton (trans.), *Cosima Wagner's Diaries. Volume II 1878–1883* (New York and London, 1980), p. 45.

13 Ibid., p. 705.

14 Ibid., p. 502.

15 Weingartner's book *Ratschläge für Aufführungen der Symphonien Beethovens* first appeared in 1906. An English translation by J. Crosland is included in *Weingartner on Music and Conducting* (New York, 1969), pp. 59–234; the essay on the *Pastoral Symphony*, pp. 141–51.

16 R. L. Smith (trans. and ed.), *Debussy on Music* (London, 1977), pp. 117–18.

17 Grove, *Beethoven and His Nine Symphonies*, pp. 182–227.

18 D. F. Tovey, *Essays in Musical Analysis. Volume I: Symphonies*, pp. 45–6.

Select bibliography

Anderson, Emily (ed.). *The Letters of Beethoven* (London, 1961)

Biba, Otto. 'Beethoven und die "Liebhaber Concerte" in Wien im Winter 1807/08' in *Beiträge '76–78: Beethoven Kolloquium 1977: Dokumentation und Aufführungspraxis*, ed. R. Klein (Kassel, 1978), pp. 82–93

'Concert Life in Beethoven's Vienna' in *Beethoven, Performers, and Critics*, ed. Robert Winter and Bruce Carr (Detroit, 1980), pp. 77–93

Bockholdt, Rudolf. *Beethoven. VI. Symphonie F-Dur op. 68 Pastorale* (Munich, 1981)

Brandenburg, Sieghard. 'Die Stichvorlage zur Erstausgabe von Beethovens Pastoralsymphonie op. 68, eine neuaufgefundene Primärquelle' in *Festschrift Rudolph Elvers zum Geburtstag*, ed. E. Herttrich and H. Schneider (Tutzing, 1985), pp. 49–61

Brandenburg, Sieghard and Martella Gutiérrez-Denhoff. *Beethoven und Böhmen. Beiträge zu Biographie und Wirkungsgeschichte Beethovens* (Bonn, 1988)

Brown, Clive. 'The Orchestra in Beethoven's Vienna', *Early Music*, 16 (1988), pp. 4–20

Comini, Alessandra. *The Changing Image of Beethoven. A Study in Mythmaking* (New York, 1987)

Cooper, Barry. *Beethoven and the Creative Process* (Oxford, 1990)

(ed.). *The Beethoven Compendium. A Guide to Beethoven's Life and Music* (London, 1991)

Forbes, Elliot (rev. and ed.). *Thayer's Life of Beethoven* (Princeton, New Jersey, 1967)

Gossett, Philip. 'Beethoven's Sixth Symphony: Sketches for the First Movement', *Journal of the American Musicological Society*, 27 (1974), pp. 248–84

Grove, George. *Beethoven and His Nine Symphonies* (London, 1896)

Jander, Owen. 'The Prophetic Conversation in Beethoven's "Scene by the Brook"', *Musical Quarterly*, 77 (1993), pp. 508–59; also an erratum published as 'The Most Meaningful Single Note in Beethoven's "Scene by the Brook". (A Meditation Inspired by a Misprint)', *Musical Quarterly*, 78 (1994), pp. 171–4

Johnson, Douglas, Alan Tyson and Robert Winter. *The Beethoven Sketchbooks* (Oxford, 1985)

Kahl, Willi. 'Zu Beethovens Naturauffassung' in *Beethoven und die Gegenwart*, ed. A. Schmitz (Berlin and Bonn, 1937), pp. 220-337

Kerman, Joseph. 'Beethoven's Sketchbooks in the British Museum', *Proceedings of the Royal Musical Association*, 93 (1966-7), pp. 77-96

Kirby, F. E. 'Beethoven's Pastoral Symphony as a *Sinfonia Caracteristica*', *Musical Quarterly*, 56 (1970), pp. 605-23

Kojima, Shin Augustinus. 'Probleme im Notentext der Pastoralsymphonie Op. 68 von Beethoven', *Beethoven Jahrbuch*, 9 (1977), pp. 217-61

Landon, H. C. Robbins (ed.). *Beethoven: A Documentary Study* (London, 1970)

Morrow, Mary Sue. *Concert Life in Haydn's Vienna: Aspects of a Developing Musical and Social Institution* (Stuyvesant, New York, 1989)

'Of Unity and Passion: The Aesthetics of Concert Criticism in Early Nineteenth-Century Vienna', *19th Century Music*, 13 (1990), pp. 193-206

Sandberger, Adolf. 'Zu den Geschichtlichen Voraussetzungen der Beethoven'schen Pastoralsinfonie', *Bulletin de la Société 'Union Musicologique'*, 3 (1923), pp. 133-85

Schindler, Anton Felix. *Beethoven as I Knew Him*. Edited by Donald W. MacArdle, translated by Constance S. Jolly (London, 1966)

Solomon, Maynard. *Beethoven* (London, 1977)

Tovey, Donald Francis. 'Beethoven. Sixth Symphony in F major (Sinfonia Pastorale), Op. 68' in *Essays in Musical Analysis. Volume I. Symphonies* (London, 1935), pp. 44-56

Tyson, Alan. 'A Reconstruction of the Pastoral Symphony Sketchbook (British Museum Add. MS 31766)' in *Beethoven Studies 1* ed. Alan Tyson (London, 1974)

Volek, Tomislav and Jaroslav Macek, 'Beethoven's Rehearsals at the Lobkowitz's', *Musical Times*, 127 (1986), pp. 75-80

Wade, Rachel W. 'Beethoven's Eroica Sketchbook', *Fontes Artis Musicae*, 23 (1976), pp. 254-89

Weise, Dagmar (ed.). *Beethoven. Ein Skizzenbuch zur Pastoralsymphonie Op. 68 und zu den Trios Op. 70, 1 und 2* (Bonn, 1961)

(ed.). *Ein Skizzenbuch zur Chorfantasie op. 80 und zu anderen Werken* (Bonn, 1957)

Index

Allgemeine musikalische Zeitung, 5, 10, 35, 37, 43–6, 50, 84
Altmann, Wilhelm, 25
Archduke Rudolph, 7–8, 20, 42, 44, 93
Artaria, 92
Auernhammer, Josepha, 4
Augarten, 4, 39

Bach, J. S., 15; Christmas Oratorio, 14
Baden, 20, 34
Bechstein, J. M., 20–1
Beeke, I., 16, 32
Beethoven, Ludwig van
love of nature, 19–22, 34
Pastoral Symphony
first movement, 12, 17, 27, 29, 36–8, 49–50, 54–61, 77, 85
second movement, 11, 17, 23, 25–6, 30, 36–8, 48–50, 61–7, 81, 83, 85, 87, 94
third movement, 12, 14, 17, 27, 30, 37, 48–50, 61, 67–73, 85
fourth movement, 12, 14, 17, 23, 29–30, 36–7, 48–50, 73–6, 83, 85–7
fifth movement, 12–14, 23, 30, 38–9, 43, 48–50, 61, 77–80, 85–6, 89
dedication, 8
early performances, 1–3, 22, 41–3, 45
early reception, 3, 43–6, 65, 81
editions, ix–x
manuscript sources, ix, 16, 41, 43–5, 60, 62, 67–8, 71, 80, 89

metronome markings, 43, 54, 61, 67, 72–3, 77
publication, ix, 39–41, 43–5, 62
sketches, 25–34, 36–8, 42, 50, 60, 64, 67, 73, 75
title, 16, 29, 31–33, 42–3, 89
other works
'Ah! perfido' (Op. 65), 2
Bacchus (sketch), 51
Bagatelle in F (Op. 33, No. 3), 22
Ballet: *Die Geschöpfe des Prometheus* (Op. 43), 22–3
Ballet: *Ritterballet* (WoO 1), 72
Cello Sonata in A (Op. 69), 30, 40
Choral Fantasia (Op. 80), 3, 42–3
Christus am Oelberge (Op. 85), 2, 6, 11, 25, 27
Coriolan overture (Op. 62), 5, 8, 27–8, 33, 39
'Die Ehre Gottes aus der Natur' (Op. 48, No. 4), 24
Fantasy in G minor (Op. 77), 2
'Gottes Macht und Vorsehung' (Op. 48, No. 5), 24
Grosse Fuge (Op. 133), 74
*Leonore (*opera) (Op. 72), 2, 8, 25, 27, 80
Leonore overtures (Op. 72), 30, 32
Macbeth (sketches), 40
'Maigesang' (Op. 52, No. 4), 23
Mass in C (Op. 86), 2, 27–32, 40, 44, 49
'Mödling' dances (WoO 17), 71
Missa Solemnis (Op. 123), 22, 28–9

Pastorella in C (attrib.), 16
Piano Concerto No. 1 (Op. 15), 5
Piano Concerto No. 3 (Op. 37), 6,
28, 39
Piano Concerto No. 4 (Op. 58), 2,
8, 27–8, 54
Piano Concerto No. 5 (Op. 73), 28
Piano Sonata in C minor (Op. 13)
(*Sonate pathétique*), 32–3
Piano Sonata in D (Op. 28) ('Pas-
toral'), 23
Piano Sonata in E♭ (Op. 81a) (*Das
Lebewohl, Abwesenheit und
Wiedersehen*), 33
Piano Sonata in C (Op. 53)
('Waldstein'), 25, 27
Piano Sonata in F minor (Op. 57)
('Appassionata'), 92
Piano Sonata in A (Op. 101), 22
Piano Sonata in B♭ (Op. 106),
('Hammerklavier'), 74
Piano Sonata in C minor (Op.
111), 74
Piano Sonatas (WoO 47), 18
Piano Trios (Op. 70), 40
Prometheus overture (Op. 43), 4–5
Quartets (Op. 18), 8
Quartets (Op. 59) ('Razumovsky'),
92
Quartetto Serioso (Op. 95), 33
Quintet for piano and wind (Op.
16), 6
Romulus und Remus (sketch), 51
'Das Rosenband' (sketch), 26
Septet (Op. 20), 6, 11, 22, 43, 62
Symphony No. 1 (Op. 21), 5–6,
8–9, 51–2, 54, 56
Symphony No. 2 (Op. 36), 5–6, 8,
51, 54, 62, 68
Symphony No. 3 (Op. 55) (*Eroica
Symphony*), 5, 7–8, 10, 20, 24–7,
32–3, 35–6, 51, 54, 59, 61,
68–9, 83
Symphony No. 4 (Op. 60), 5, 8,
20, 27–8, 39, 45, 51, 54, 68
Symphony No. 5 (Op. 67), 2–3,

24–5, 27, 30, 40–3, 45, 48,
50–51, 53–4, 61, 68–9, 80
Symphony No. 7 (Op. 92), 40, 50
Symphony No. 8 (Op. 93), 52
Symphony No. 9 (Op. 125)
('Choral'), 50, 61, 86
Triple Concerto (Op. 56), 8, 25,
27, 39
Variations on 'Là ci darem la
mano' (WoO 28), 6
Vestas Feuer (Hess 115), 25
Violin Concerto (Op. 61), 27–8, 45
Violin Sonata in F (Op. 24)
('Spring'), 23
'Vom Tode' (Op. 48, No. 3), 26
'Der Wachtelschlag' (WoO 129),
23–4
'Zur Erde sank die Ruh' von
Himmel nieder' (sketch), 26
Beethoven-Gesamtausgabe, ix
Berlioz, Hector, 83–4
Symphonie Fantastique, 47, 82–3
Bethlehem, 16
Biba, Otto, 93
Bigot, Marie, 19
birdsong, 11–12, 15, 18, 23–4, 36–7, 62,
65–7, 83
Böck, Anton, 53
Böck, Ignaz, 53
Bohdanowicz family, 36
Bonaparte, Jerome (King of West-
phalia), 42
Bossler, 18
Boswell, 65
Böttger, Adolf, 82
Brauchle, J. X., 20
Breitkopf and Härtel, ix, 19–20, 29,
39–41, 44–5, 92
Brixi, F. X., 15
Broderip and Wilkinson, 23
Bureau des Arts et d'Industrie, 2
Burgtheater, 6, 39, 41–4

Cäcilia, 82
Cannabich, C., 16
Charlton, David, 94

Cherubini, L., 7, 9
Chew, Geoffrey, 16
Collin, Heinrich, 30, 40
Concert Lamoureux, 86
Cooper, Barry, 27
Corelli, A; Christmas Concerto, 14
Czerny, C., 4, 34
  Die Kunst der älteren und neueren
    Klaviercompositionen, 28

D'Agoult, Marie, 84
Debussy, Claude, 54, 86–7
Del Mar, Norman, 94
Dittersdorf, C., 7, 16, 19, 92
  Ovid symphonies, 17
Dornbach, 38
Düsseldorf, 84
dynamic markings, 48, 56–7, 60, 69, 73,
    75, 77–8

Eberl, A., 7, 9–10
  Symphony in D minor, 10
  Symphony in E♭, 10
Eberlin, J. E., 15
Eisenberg, 7
Eisenstadt, 2
Emperor Franz, 7
Engel, Johann Jacob, 35
Eroica Sketchbook, 25–7, 31, 72
Esterházy, Prince Nicolaus, 7
Esterházy, Prince Nicolaus (II), 28
Esterházy, Princess Marie
    Hermenegild, 28, 30
Eulenburg, ix, 25, 92
Eybler, J. L., 9

Fantasia (film), 87
Fétis, F–J., 18
folkmusic, 16, 77
Fontenelle, 35
Fränzel, F., 9
  Bird Song Symphony, 36
Freunde der Tonkunst, 54
Fuchs, J. L., 28

Gaden, 72

Galeazzi, F., 51
Gardiner, John Eliot, x
Gellert, C. F., 24, 26
Gerber, E. L., 53
Gesellschaft der Associirten, 8, 10
Gesellschaft der Musikfreunde, 43–4,
    93
Gesellschaft von Musikfreunden, 5
Glacis, 20
Glass, Philip, 59
Gluck, C. W.
  Alceste overture, 32
Goethe, J. W., 21
  Propyläen, 15
Gossett, Philip, 59
Grétry, A–E–M., 51
Grinzing, 65
Grove, George, 76, 87–8
  Beethoven and his Nine Symphonies,
    88
Gyrowetz, A., 9

Hamburg, 21, 82
Handel, G. F., 15
  Acis and Galatea, 76, 84
  Messiah, 14
Hänsel, 8
harmonic rhythm, 56–9, 61, 63, 77,
    79–80
harmonic vocabulary, 49, 57, 59–61,
    63, 73–5, 77, 79–80
Härtel, G. C., 41
Haydn, Joseph, 5, 7, 9–10, 14, 16,
    18–19, 28, 38, 45–8, 93
  The Creation, 5, 7–8, 10–12, 14, 24,
    30–31, 35–8, 49, 51, 54, 74–5,
    88, 94
  'Harmoniemesse', 28
  London Symphonies, 51
  Missa Sancti Nicolai, 16, 29
  Quartet in G (Op. 76, No. 1), 50
  Quartet in C (Op. 76, No. 3)
    ('Emperor'), 50
  Il ritorno di Tobia, 43
  The Seasons, 8, 10–14, 23, 35, 37–8,
    45–6, 51, 54, 77, 94

The Seven Last Words, 11
Symphonies Nos. 6, 7, 8 (*Le matin, Le midi, Le soir*), 17
Symphony No. 45 ('Farewell'), 17, 47
Symphony No. 67, 52
Symphony No. 79, 52
Symphony No. 89, 52
Symphony No. 97, 52
Haydn, Michael, 16, 18
Heiligenstadt, 20, 38–9, 65
Heine, 82
Hetzendorf, 20
Hoffmeister, F. A., 9
Symphony in F (*La primavera*), 17
Hofmann, L., 16, 32
Hollywood, 87
Homer, 21
horn, 51, 53, 80, 86
Hummel, J. N., 28

Jander, Owen, 65, 91, 94

Kaltenleutgeben, 72
Kanne, 9
Karnavich, 9
Kauer, 9
Killitzky, 1
Kinsky, Prince, 8, 42
Kirby, F. E., 32
Kirnberger, 51
Kloeber, August von, 20
Klopstock, 26, 51
Klumpar, 41
Knecht, J. H., 51
Le portrait musical de la nature, 18–19
Kozeluch, J. A., 15
Kramer, 9
Krommer, F.; *Sestetto Pastorale*, 94

Laab, 72
Landon, Else Radant, 93
Landsberg 10 sketchbook, 33–4, 36–8
Lefèvre, Xavier; *Hymne a l'Agriculture*, 94
Leipzig, 4, 39, 44–5

Leopoldstadt Theatre, 36
Lichnowsky, 7
Liebhaber Concerte, 5–6, 8–9, 30, 36, 42
Liszt, Franz, 84
Ce qu'on entend sur la montagne, 84
Lobkowitz, Prince Joseph Franz Maximilian, 7–8, 10, 30, 41–3
London, 4, 84
Ludwig van Beethoven: Werke: Neue Ausgabe sämtlicher Werke, x
Lyons, 84
Lyser, J. P., 82

Magdeburg, 21
Mahler, G., 47
Malfatti, Therese, 19
Marston, Nicholas, 91
Martini, 9
Marx, Adolf Bernhard, 91
Mayer, 36
Mayseder, 9
Mehlgrube, 5
Michelangelo, 83
Mödling, 20, 70–1
Monteverdi, C., 15
Moscheles, I., 9, 94
Mosengeil, Friedrich, 81–2
Mozart, L; Symphony in D (*Die Bauernhochzeit*), 17
Toy Symphony, 18
Mozart, W. A., 4–5, 7, 9–10, 16, 19, 47
Così fan tutte, 8
Davidde penitente, 44
Die Entführung aus dem Serail, 8
Don Giovanni overture, 32
'Exsultate, jubilate', 52
Symphony in F (K. 130), 52
Symphony in C (K. 425) ('Linz'), 52
Müller, 9
Musikalisches Institut, 5
Mysliveček, J., 17

Napoleonic wars, 5–6, 9, 19
Neate, Charles, 34
Nohant, 84

Norrington, Roger, ix
Nottebohm, Gustav, 25
Nussdorf, 20
Nyman, Michael, 59

Oberglogau, 30
Oppersdorff, Count, 30, 41–2, 92

Paer, 8
Palestrina, G. P., 15
Paris, 4, 86
pastoral mass, 15–16, 29, 51
pastoral music, 14–16, 22–4, 56–7
pastoral symphony, 16, 31–2
Pastoral Symphony Sketchbook, 30–3
pastorella, 16, 51
piccolo, 52–3
Pichl, W., 7
Poussin, 83
Prague, 7, 30
programme symphony, 17–19

ranz des vaches, 77, 79
Razumovsky, Count, 8, 41
Riemann, Hugo, 71
Ries, F., 41
Rietz, Julius, ix
Rigi, 77
Rösner, 9
Roudnice (Raudnitz), 7
Rubinstein, Anton, 85
Rust, Wilhelm, 92

St Marx Bürgerspital, 6
St Petersburg, 10
Der Sammler, 43–4
Sand, George, 84
Sandberger, Adolf, 14–15
Schacht, 9
scherzo, 47–8, 68–9
Schindler, A. F., 21, 34, 50, 64–6,
   70–2
Schleinitz, 85
Schoenberg, Arnold, 57
Schönfeld, Count, 39
Schubart, D., 51

Schubert, Franz; Die schöne Müllerin,
   94
Schumann, Robert, 82
   Symphony No. 1 (Op. 38) ('Spring'),
   82
Schuppanzigh, Ignaz, 4
Seyfried, Ignaz von, 9, 43
Shakespeare, 21, 40
sinfonia caracteristica, 32–3, 35
Spohr, L., 82
Stamitz, J., 16
Stein, Friedrich, 39
Stein, Heinrich von, 85
Steiner, 43
Stokowski, L., 87
storm movements, 12, 15, 17–19, 23, 48
Struck, 9
Sturm, C. C., 21–2, 24
Swieten, Gottfried van, 8

Thayer, A. W., 34
Theater an der Wien, 1, 4, 6, 9, 22, 42,
   44, 88
Theocritus, 83
timpani, 15, 23, 51–3, 86
Tomášek, 9
tonal structure, 49–50, 69, 75
tone painting, 11–14, 17–19, 33–7,
   42–3, 45–6, 66–7, 71, 76, 81–2,
   87–8
Tonkünstler–Societät, 6, 43, 44
Tovey, Donald, 65–6, 69, 87–8
Traeg, Johann, 18
trombones, 51–3
trumpets, 15, 51–2, 72, 86
Türk, D. G., 32

Universal Edition, ix
University of Vienna, 5

Vanhal, J. B., 7, 15–16, 19
   Symphony in C, 17
   Symphony in E♭, 17
Vaterländische Blätter, 8
Virgil, 83
Vivaldi, A., 15

Flute Concerto (Op. 10, No. 3)
  (RV 428) ('Il gardellino'), 65
The Seasons, 14
Vogler, Abbé, 8–9, 37, 48, 51
  Invocation to the sun at midnight in Lapland, 36
  The Shepherds' Joy interrupted by a thunderstorm, 36
  The Siege of Jericho, 36, 47
Vienna; concert life, 1–8

Wade, Rachel W., 25
Wagner, Cosima, 85
Wagner, Richard, 85–6
waterscapes, 11, 15, 17–18, 62
Webster, James, 90

Wegeler, F. G., 19
Weingartner, Felix, 86
Wigand, Balthasar, 30–31
Winter, P., 7
Wohlthätigkeitsanstalten, 6, 39
Wordsworth, 33
Wranitzky, A., 7, 43
Wranitzky, P.; *Grand Sinfonie Caractéristique pour la paix avec la République Française*, 33
Würth, Baron, 7–8

Zeitung für die elegante Welt, 81
Zimmerman, A., 16
  Symphony (*Pastoritia*), 18